THE SCIENCE TIMELINE WALLBOOK

SKY & SPACE

TRANSPORT & COMMS

BUILDING & INVENTION

EARTH & LAND

MEDICINE & BIOLOGY

PHYSICS & CHEMISTRY

MATH & MEASUREMENT

585 BC – Thales of Miletus, the first Western philosopher, astonishes contemporaries by correctly predicting a solar eclipse will take place on May 28, 585 BC. He uses Babylonian records of movements of the Sun and Moon to work out the timings of solar and lunar eclipses. He also introduces geometry to Ancient Greece.

140 BC – Greek astronomer Hipparchus invents the astrolabe, a machine that measures the angle of the Sun or a star above the horizon. Astrolabes are used to predict the positions of the Sun, Moon, and planets to determine local time and latitude.

150 AD – Ancient philosopher Ptolemy's book *Almagest* describes the Universe with the Earth as its middle point to account for the movements of the Sun, Moon, … It is popular … st- … my.

1500 BC – An alphabet of 22 symbols emerges in Phoenicia (in the Near East) from which all Western alphabets are descended. The system makes it easier for traders to read and write.

270 BC – Greek astronomer Aristarchus comes to the startling conclusion that the Earth is in orbit around the Sun. Most people do not take his idea seriously.

… simple paper hot-air balloon, now called a Kongming lantern, to signal his position when surrounded by enemies.

250 AD – Chinese scientist Ma Jun desig… wheeled south-pointing chariot, with th… first differential gears. The chariot acts li… to help direct troops in the dark.

2.6 million years ago – Early humans pound fist-sized pieces of stone to fashion sharp edges into blades for cutting flesh, skinning hides, and crafting into spearheads.

700 BC – Windmills are developed in China to pump water and in Persia to grind grain.

200 BC – Apollonius of Perga, a Greek astronomer, explains the movement of planets after studying the properties of cones, giving names to the parabola, ellipse, and hyperbola.

105 AD – Official Cai Lun gets credit for inventing paper by boiling a mixture of mulberry tree bark, hemp, old linens, and fish nets into a pulp, but really it existed 200 years earlier. The Chinese use it for making everything from kites to playing cards.

25,000 BC – Sewing needles made from bone enable people to make clothes that provide insulation and comfort.

3500 BC – Egyptians use square sails to propel boats upstream, making the Nile River a two-way superhighway.

800 BC – Greeks are intrigued by an iron-attracting mineral they find in the district of Magnesia and discover magnetism.

150 BC – Pergamun, Turkey, becomes a center for making parchment from scrubbed animal skin as an alternative to increasingly rare papyrus.

100 AD – Hero of Alexandria describes what is thought to be the first steam engine, an aeolipile. It has a rocket-style jet engine with nozzles that spin when heated.

231 AD – Strategist Zhuge Liang issues the recently invented wheelbarrow to Chinese soldiers to transport supplies. It is probably not used in Europe for another 1,000 years.

3000 BC – Sumerian merchants mark transactions on clay tablets and bake them to make the inscriptions permanent. Priests write down the movements of the planets and rulers send written laws across their domains.

250 BC – *"Give me a lever long enough, and I shall move the world!"* Greek genius Archimedes describes a screw for pumping water and builds a system of pulleys, fulcrums, gears, and levers to launch the giant ship *Syracusia* (4,064 tons) single-handedly, without an army of slaves.

15 BC – Roman engineer Marcus Vitruvius writes *De Architectura,* a 10-volume treatise on architecture.

50 AD – Roman engineers develop the *polyspastos*, a giant human-powered crane worked by four men on a treadmill. It can lift loads of more than six tons and is used for constructing amphitheaters and aqueducts.

10,000 BC – Early farmers build huts to stop produce going rotten and to protect animals from attack. Food is sold at markets, leading to the rise of towns and cities.

6000 BC – Farmers develop axes with handles, capable of chopping down trees to allow sunlight to reach crops. Tree felling intensifies as civilizations emerge, creating pasture for animals, and space and raw materials for building markets, towns, and cities.

500 BC – Greeks observe the strange attracting force of static electricity when amber (known as *electron*) is rubbed against cloth.

64 AD – Concrete becomes the preferred building material across the Roman Empire.

3000 BC – Brickmakers in the Middle East place blocks of clay, sand, and water into kilns and bake them at over 3600°F. Fired bricks enable the first truly permanent, weatherproof structures to be built.

300 BC – Greek author Theophrastus writes *On the History of Plants*, the earliest surviving botanical work. It classifies plants in groups and describes how to graft plants.

3500 BC – An unknown genius in Europe or the Middle East invents the wheel with the ingenious idea of fixing two potter's wheels on an axle, which in turn is fixed to a sled, to form the first cart.

300 BC – Greek polymath Dicaearchus of Messana compiles a map of the world containing two lines of reference, an idea that later becomes longitude and latitude.

20 BC – Antipater of Thessalonica refers to a watermill harnessing water flow to grind grain.

31 AD – Du-Shi, a Prefect of Nanyang, uses hydraulic (water-powered) bellows to increase the heat of a blast furnace. Chinese people use cast iron for making plows for heavy soil.

STONE AGE	-5K	-1K	-500	-300	-200	-100	0	100	200	300

14,000 BC – Fired clay pots (Jomon ware) appear in Japan, making it easy to boil food. After the birth of agriculture in the Near East, ca. 10,000 years ago, pottery spreads worldwide and is used for cooking and storage.

5500 BC – The scratch-plow is deployed by farmers in Mesopotamia and the Indus Valley to prepare the soil for seeds to be sown.

570 BC – Anaximander of Miletus concludes all life began in the sea.

330 BC – Greek philosopher Aristotle, who writes scientific works on animals, plants, and the Universe, establishes that scientific theory should be derived from observation. For example, he concludes that the world is round after noting that stars in the southern and northern hemispheres are different, a phenomenon only explained by the curvature of the Earth.

150 BC – Stirrups, invented in Asia, enable horseback riders to use bigger weapons without falling off.

132 AD – Chinese scholar Zhang Heng creates the first machine to detect earthquakes. His urn-like seismological detector drops one of eight balls from a dragon's mouth to indicate when and in what direction an earthquake has occurred.

150 AD – The multiple-tube iron seed drill is invented in China. It allows seeds to be sown rapidly in straight rows, instead of being scattered randomly by hand.

2500 BC – Sumerian farmers sprinkle sulfur on their fields to ward off insects, rodents, and fungi—the first use of pesticides.

400 BC – Hippocrates of Cos claims diseases are caused naturally and are not simply the whims of gods. His followers produce more than 70 works, including *The Hippocratic Oath*—still taken by doctors today—which obliges physicians to ensure patient confidentiality and the highest ethics.

3000 BC – Molten copper and tin are mixed to make bronze by metallurgists in India, China, and the Middle East. Bronze makes spoked wheels, tougher weapons, and tools.

380 BC – Polybus, a pupil of Hippocrates, suggests that poor health and illness are caused by a deficiency or excess of four bodily humors: black bile, blood, yellow bile, and phlegm. The idea underpins the practice of bloodletting, which remains commonplace in Europe until the late 19th century.

50 BC – Phoenician artisans discover how to make intricate objects by attaching a blob of molten glass onto a long hollow tube through which they blow a bubble of air. Glass blowing spreads rapidly across the Roman Empire.

158 AD – Roman physician Galen of Pergamon writes about health and medicine from his experience working with wounded gladiators and dissecting monkeys and pigs. He establishes the brain, and not the heart, controls the nervous system. Galen's works are taught in Europe until the 19th century.

The discovery of how to light and control fire about one million years ago makes humans the most powerful species on Earth. Fire means early people can scare off wild animals, keep warm in cooler regions, and cook food, which is safer and easier to digest than uncooked food. Fire underpins science and engineering, from forging Bronze Age tools to the manufacturing of modern industrial chemicals.

400 BC – Democritus develops a radical idea that all matter is made up of indivisible atoms of varying shapes and sizes, a theory revived 2,200 years later by John Dalton.

250 BC – It is said that Archimedes leaps from his bath shouting *eureka* ("I have found it"), upon realizing a body immersed in fluid experiences an upthrust equal to the weight of fluid displaced.

250 AD – Alchemists working in Alexandria are also the world's first experimental chemists. Their legendary founder, Hermes Trismegistus, claimed to have discovered the secret of the philosopher's stone, which can turn lead into gold.

3000 BC – Candles, made from beeswax and papyrus wicks, are developed in Ancient Egypt.

200 AD – Pagan, Christian, and Jewish alchemists, based at the school of Greek philosopher Ammonius Saccas in Alexandria, compile a body of mystical writings called the *Hermetica*. They provide inspiration for philosophers and alchemists seeking to turn lead into gold through chemical experimentation.

20,000 BC – Weapons that allow people to kill beyond throwing range give a huge boost to humanity's control of nature. The bow is the first machine to store energy, while arrows with sharpened arrowheads and feather shafts are lethal and accurate.

3000 BC – As an alternative to flatbread, Egyptian bakers use yeast added to flour, to make light loaves.

450 BC – Empedocles, a Greek philosopher living in Sicily, states that all matter is made up of four elemental substances—earth, fire, air, and water. His theory is widely accepted for more than 2,000 years.

529 BC – Pythagoras of Samos establishes a school of philosophy that proves that in any right-angled triangle the square of the longest side is equal to the sum of the squares of the other two. He also establishes a link in music between the length of a string and its harmonic pitch.

240 BC – Greek Eratosthenes calculates the circumference of the Earth to an accuracy of 96% by measuring shadows cast at noon on the summer solstice at two different locations in Egypt.

45 BC – Julius Caesar's new calendar is introduced at a time when its predecessor (see 432 BC—Meton) has become out of step with the seasons by three months.

300 AD – Mayans living in Central America pioneer a counting system based on the numbers 20 and 5, including a symbol for zero (represented by a shell). Their calendar, based on a complicated series of annual cycles, is still used in some areas of Guatemala and Mexico.

432 BC – Meton of Athens devises a calendar to keep lunar months in line with the seasons. The 19-year cycle features 12 years of 12 lunar months and 7 years of 13 lunar months.

1000 BC – Egyptian water clocks measure time without the Sun. Water flows evenly from one funnel-shaped vessel into another.

300 BC – Euclid of Alexandria defines five basic axioms from which all geometric proofs are made. *The Elements* remains one of the standard textbooks on geometry.

50 BC – The *Antikythera Mechanism* is manufactured by an unknown Greek engineering genius. It contains more than 30 cogs and gears that compute movements of the Sun, Moon, and planets. Similar devices do not reappear until the first mechanical clocks are devised in China and Islamic Spain more than 1,000 years later.

250 AD – Diophantus of Alexandria writes a series of mathematical books called *Arithmetica*, the first to deal with algebra.

490 AD – Indian mathematician Aryabhata calculates the Earth's circumference to an accuracy of 99.8%.

3000 BC – Babylonians devise a counting system based on the number 60, establishing divisions for the time of day (60 seconds and 60 minutes) and degrees of angles (360° in a circle).

1000 BC – Merchants' counting boards used in China and the Middle East develop into a calculating aid known as an abacus. In China counting rods are mounted on boards.

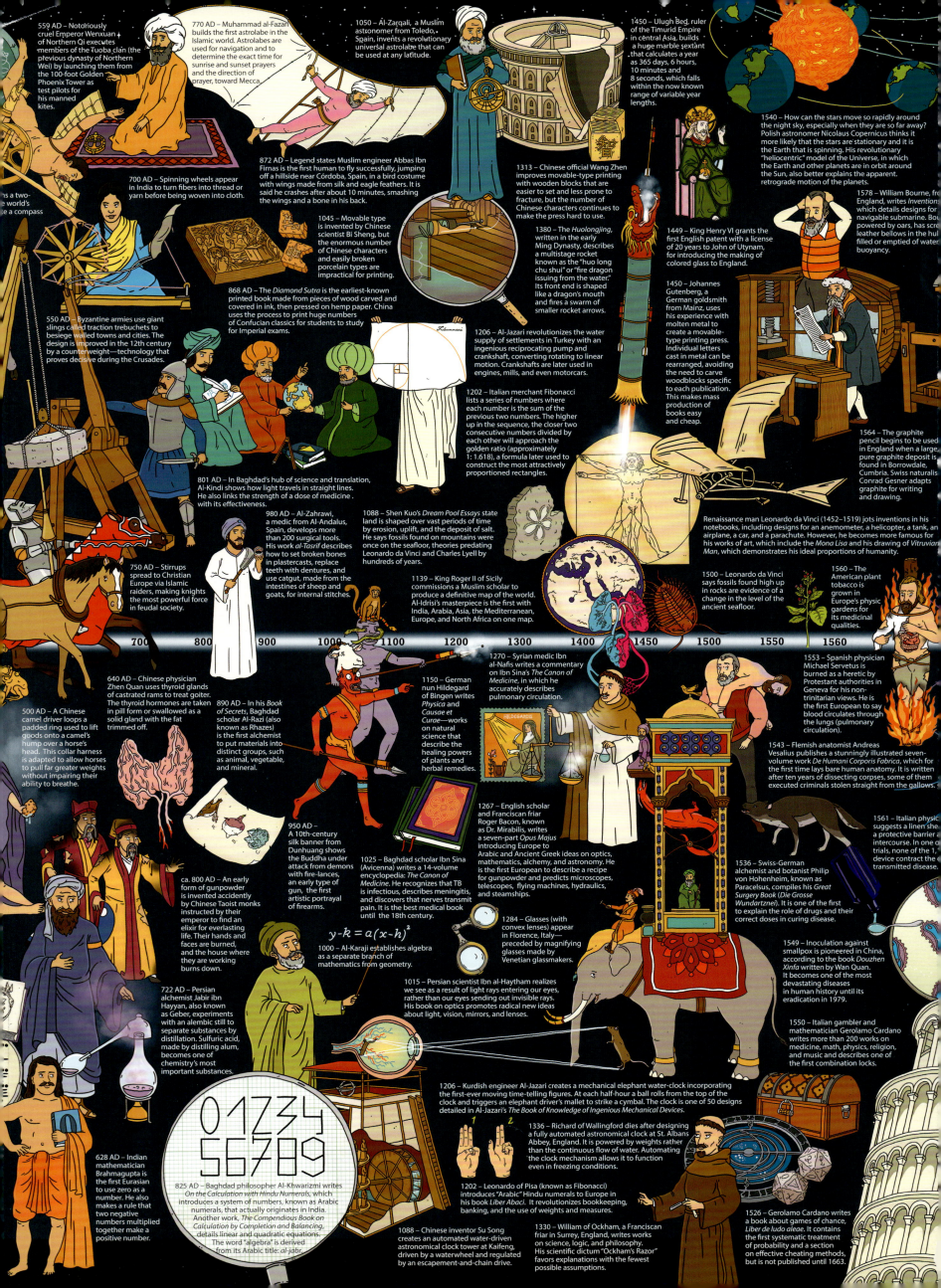

559 AD – Notoriously cruel Emperor Wenxuan of Northern Qi executes members of the Tuoba clan (the previous dynasty of Northern Wei) by launching them from the 100-foot Golden Phoenix Tower as test pilots for his manned kites.

770 AD – Muhammad al-Fazari builds the first astrolabe in the Islamic world. Astrolabes are used for navigation and to determine the exact time for sunrise and sunset prayers and the direction of prayer, toward Mecca.

1050 – Al-Zarqali, a Muslim astronomer from Toledo, Spain, invents a revolutionary universal astrolabe that can be used at any latitude.

1450 – Ulugh Beg, ruler of the Timurid Empire in central Asia, builds a huge marble sextant that calculates a year as 365 days, 6 hours, 10 minutes and 8 seconds, which falls within the now known range of variable year lengths.

1540 – How can the stars move so rapidly around the night sky, especially when they are so far away? Polish astronomer Nicolaus Copernicus thinks it more likely that the stars are stationary and it is the Earth that is spinning. His revolutionary "heliocentric" model of the Universe, in which the Earth and other planets are in orbit around the Sun, also better explains the apparent retrograde motion of the planets.

700 AD – Spinning wheels appear in India to turn fibers into thread or yarn before being woven into cloth.

872 AD – Legend states Muslim engineer Abbas Ibn Firnas is the first human to fly successfully, jumping off a hillside near Córdoba, Spain, in a bird costume with wings made from silk and eagle feathers. It is said he crashes after about 10 minutes, smashing the wings and a bone in his back.

1313 – Chinese official Wang Zhen improves movable-type printing with wooden blocks that are easier to set and less prone to traction, but the number of Chinese characters continues to make the press hard to use.

1449 – King Henry VI grants the first English patent with a license of 20 years to John of Utynam, for introducing the making of colored glass to England.

1578 – William Bourne, fr. England, writes Invention which details designs for navigable submarine. Bo powered by oars, has scr leather bellows in the hul filled or emptied of water buoyancy.

ns a two... world's ...a compass

1045 – Movable type is invented by Chinese scientist Bi Sheng, but the enormous number of Chinese characters and easily broken porcelain types are impractical for printing.

1380 – The Huolongjing, written in the early Ming Dynasty, describes a multistage rocket known as the "huo long chu shui" or "fire dragon issuing from the water." Its front end is shaped like a dragon's mouth and fires a swarm of smaller rocket arrows.

1450 – Johannes Gutenberg, a German goldsmith from Mainz, uses his experience with molten metal to create a movable-type printing press. Individual letters cast in metal can be rearranged, avoiding the need to carve woodblocks specific to each publication. This makes mass production of books easy and cheap.

868 AD – The Diamond Sutra is the earliest-known printed book made from pieces of wood carved and covered in ink, then pressed on hemp paper. China uses the process to print huge numbers of Confucian classics for students to study for Imperial exams.

550 AD – Byzantine armies use giant slings called traction trebuchets to besiege walled towns and cities. The design is improved in the 12th century by a counterweight—technology that proves decisive during the Crusades.

1206 – Al-Jazari revolutionizes the water supply of settlements in Turkey with an ingenious reciprocating pump and crankshaft, converting rotating to linear motion. Crankshafts are later used in engines, mills, and even motorcars.

1202 – Italian merchant Fibonacci lists a series of numbers where each number is the sum of the previous two numbers. The higher up in the sequence, the closer two consecutive numbers divided by each other will approach the golden ratio (approximately 1:1.618), a formula later used to construct the most attractively proportioned rectangles.

1564 – The graphite pencil begins to be used in England when a large, pure graphite deposit is found in Borrowdale, Cumbria. Swiss naturalis Conrad Gesner adapts graphite for writing and drawing.

801 AD – In Baghdad's hub of science and translation, Al-Kindi shows how light travels in straight lines. He also links the strength of a dose of medicine with its effectiveness.

980 AD – Al-Zahrawi, a medic from Al-Andalus, Spain, develops more than 200 surgical tools. His work al-Tasrif describes how to set broken bones in plastercasts, replace teeth with dentures, and use catgut, made from the intestines of sheep and goats, for internal stitches.

1088 – Shen Kuo's Dream Pool Essays state land is shaped over vast periods of time by erosion, uplift, and the deposit of salt. He says fossils found on mountains were once on the seafloor, theories predating Leonardo da Vinci and Charles Lyell by hundreds of years.

Renaissance man Leonardo da Vinci (1452–1519) jots inventions in his notebooks, including designs for an anemometer, a helicopter, a tank, an airplane, a car, and a parachute. However, he becomes more famous for his works of art, which include the Mona Lisa and his drawing of Vitruvian Man, which demonstrates his ideal proportions of humanity.

750 AD – Stirrups spread to Christian Europe via Islamic raiders, making knights the most powerful force in feudal society.

1139 – King Roger II of Sicily commissions a Muslim scholar to produce a definitive map of the world. Al-Idrisi's masterpiece is the first with India, Arabia, Asia, the Mediterranean, Europe, and North Africa on one map.

1500 – Leonardo da Vinci says fossils found high up in rocks are evidence of a change in the level of the ancient seafloor.

1560 – The American plant tobacco is grown in Europe's physic gardens for its medicinal qualities.

700   800   900   1000   1100   1200   1300   1400   1450   1500   1550   1560

640 AD – Chinese physician Zhen Quan uses thyroid glands of castrated rams to treat goiter. The thyroid hormones are taken in pill form or swallowed as a solid gland with the fat trimmed off.

890 AD – In his Book of Secrets, Baghdad scholar Al-Razi (also known as Rhazes) is the first alchemist to put materials into distinct groups, such as animal, vegetable, and mineral.

1150 – German nun Hildegard of Bingen writes Physica and Causae et Curae—works on natural science that describe the healing powers of plants and herbal remedies.

1270 – Syrian medic Ibn al-Nafis writes a commentary on Ibn Sina's The Canon of Medicine, in which he accurately describes pulmonary circulation.

1553 – Spanish physician Michael Servetus is burned as a heretic by Protestant authorities in Geneva for his non-trinitarian views. He is the first European to say blood circulates through the lungs (pulmonary circulation).

500 AD – A Chinese camel driver loops a padded ring used to lift goods onto a camel's hump over a horse's head. This collar harness is adapted to allow horses to pull far greater weights without impairing their ability to breathe.

1543 – Flemish anatomist Andreas Vesalius publishes a stunningly illustrated seven-volume work De Humani Corporis Fabrica, which for the first time lays bare human anatomy. It is written after ten years of dissecting corpses, some of them executed criminals stolen straight from the gallows.

1561 – Italian physic suggests a linen she a protective barrier a intercourse. In one o trials, none of the 1, device contract the transmitted disease.

950 AD – A 10th-century silk banner from Dunhuang shows the Buddha under attack from demons with fire-lances, an early type of gun, the first artistic portrayal of firearms.

1025 – Baghdad scholar Ibn Sina (Avicenna) writes a 14-volume encyclopedia: The Canon of Medicine. He recognizes that TB is infectious, describes meningitis, and discovers that nerves transmit pain. It is the best medical book until the 18th century.

1267 – English scholar and Franciscan friar Roger Bacon, known as Dr. Mirabilis, writes a seven-part Opus Majus introducing European to Arabic and Ancient Greek ideas on optics, mathematics, alchemy, and astronomy. He is the first European to describe a recipe for gunpowder and predicts microscopes, telescopes, flying machines, hydraulics, and steamships.

1536 – Swiss-German alchemist and botanist Philip von Hohenheim, known as Paracelsus, compiles his Great Surgery Book (Die Grosse Wundartznei). It is one of the first to explain the role of drugs and their correct doses in curing disease.

ca. 800 AD – An early form of gunpowder is invented accidentally by Chinese Taoist monks instructed by their emperor to find an elixir for everlasting life. Their hands and faces are burned, and the house where they are working burns down.

$$y - k = a(x - h)^2$$

1000 – Al-Karaji establishes algebra as a separate branch of mathematics from geometry.

1284 – Glasses (with convex lenses) appear in Florence, Italy—preceded by magnifying glasses made by Venetian glassmakers.

1549 – Inoculation against smallpox is pioneered in China, according to the book Douzhen Xinfa written by Wan Quan. It becomes one of the most devastating diseases in human history until its eradication in 1979.

722 AD – Persian alchemist Jabir ibn Hayyan, also known as Geber, experiments with an alembic still to separate substances by distillation. Sulfuric acid, made by distilling alum, becomes one of chemistry's most important substances.

1015 – Persian scientist Ibn al-Haytham realizes we see as a result of light rays entering our eyes, rather than our eyes sending out invisible rays. His book on optics promotes radical new ideas about light, vision, mirrors, and lenses.

1550 – Italian gambler and mathematician Gerolamo Cardano writes more than 200 works on medicine, math, physics, religion, and music and describes one of the first combination locks.

1206 – Kurdish engineer Al-Jazari creates a mechanical elephant water-clock incorporating the first-ever moving time-telling figures. At each half-hour a ball rolls from the top of the clock and triggers an elephant driver's mallet to strike a cymbal. This clock is one of 50 designs detailed in Al-Jazari's The Book of Knowledge of Ingenious Mechanical Devices.

0 1 2 3 4 5 6 7 8 9

628 AD – Indian mathematician Brahmagupta is the first Eurasian to use zero as a number. He also makes a rule that two negative numbers multiplied together make a positive number.

825 AD – Baghdad philosopher Al-Khwarizmi writes On the Calculation with Hindu Numerals, which introduces a system of numbers, known as Arabic numerals, that actually originates in India. Another work, The Compendious Book on Calculation by Completion and Balancing, details linear and quadratic equations. The word "algebra" is derived from its Arabic title: al-jabr.

1336 – Richard of Wallingford dies after designing a fully automated astronomical clock at St. Albans Abbey, England. It is powered by weights rather than the continuous flow of water. Automating the clock mechanism allows it to function even in freezing conditions.

1202 – Leonardo of Pisa (known as Fibonacci) introduces "Arabic" Hindu numerals to Europe in his book Liber Abaci. It revolutionizes bookkeeping, banking, and the use of weights and measures.

1088 – Chinese inventor Su Song creates an automated water-driven astronomical clock tower at Kaifeng, driven by a waterwheel and regulated by an escapement-and-chain drive.

1330 – William of Ockham, a Franciscan friar in Surrey, England, writes works on science, logic, and philosophy. His scientific dictum "Ockham's Razor" favors explanations with the fewest possible assumptions.

1526 – Gerolamo Cardano writes a book about games of chance, Liber de ludo aleae. It contains the first systematic treatment of probability and a section on effective cheating methods, but is not published until 1663.

1572 – Danish astronomer Tycho Brahe notices a new star appear in the heavens. The supernova explosion, visible until 1574, disproves Aristotle's belief the heavens never change. Brahe later builds the observatories of Uraniborg and Stjerneborg on the island of Hven.

1609 – In Prague, German astronomer Johannes Kepler uses his master Tycho Brahe's observations to propose three new laws of planetary motion, showing planets move in elliptical rather than circular orbits.

1633 – According to legend, Turkish engineer Lagari Hasan Çelebi makes the first manned rocket. He launches himself into the air using 285 pounds of gunpowder and lands safely using a type of parachute.

1663 – Scottish mathematician James Gregory proposes a method for calculating the distance between the Earth and the Sun (known as the astronomical unit) by observing the transit of Venus across the Sun from different positions around the Earth.

1669 – Isaac Newton writes a letter to the Royal Society mentioning a new type of telescope he has developed that uses mirrors instead of lenses to focus light. His reflecting telescope avoids the problem of light dispersing and distorting images.

1705 – English astronomer Edmond determines the periodicity of a sho comet clearly visible from the Earth every 75–76 years). Ten years later the path of the Moon's shadow ove during a solar eclipse, accurate to f

1624 – King James I of England is forced to sign Parliament's Statute of Monopolies, designed to protect new inventions, and put an end to centuries of monarchs granting corrupt concessions to favorites.

1638 – Hezârfen Ahmed Çelebi successfully crosses the Bosphorus using a pair of man-made wings after launching himself from the Galata Tower. This is his tenth attempt at flight, and the first that succeeds, winning him a grand prize of 1,000 gold pieces.

1710 – In England, Abrah Staffordshire Quaker, buil Coalbrookdale, Shropshir into pig iron using coke (place of charcoal (made f or poured, pig iron turns essential material for brid many inventions of the Ir

n Kent, nd Devices e first e's boat, powered hat are control

1634 – Galileo experiments using a ramp to roll balls down a slope. He discovers the distance traveled by a falling body is proportional to the square of the time of travel—i.e. it undergoes constant acceleration.

1662 – Blaise Pascal devises the first public bus service in Paris, with fixed schedules, routes, and fares.

1691 – Edmond Halley builds a diving bell, complete with an external window for underwater exploration. He plunges it 60 feet deep into the River Thames, and remains inside (with five friends!) for more than 90 minutes.

1610 – Galileo improves telescopes, achieving a 30x magnification. He discovers Jupiter has moons, disproving the traditional view all celestial objects orbit the Earth. Galileo's support for Copernicus's theory that the Earth orbits the Sun, not vice versa, leads him into conflict with the Catholic Church. He is sentenced to house arrest for heresy until his death in 1642.

1644 – René Descartes' famous phrase cogito ergo sum ("I think therefore I am") appears in his book Principles of Philosophy.

1712 – Thomas Newcomen, a Devon, England, invents the fi engine. Newcomen markets h Savery's patent, covering mac by fire. It is used to pump wat out of tin mines.

1620 – Dutch inventor Cornelius Drebbel builds the first working submarine and holds trials in the river Thames, England. It is powered by oars and is shown off to a large, admiring crowd flanking the river, including King James I.

1629 – Designs for a basic steam engine are shown in the book Le Machine written by Italian inventor Giovanni Branca.

1662 – English scientists are given a royal charter by King Charles II and become known as the Royal Society. English polymath Robert Hooke is its first curator of experiments. The society's motto is nullius in verba ("take nobody's word for it").

1676 – Dutch scientist and microscope maker Antonie Van Leeuwenhoek discovers bacteria, sperm, protozoa, and other microscopic lifeforms, calling them "animalcules."

1698 – Thomas Savery, a military engineer from Devon, England, lodges a patent for a basic piston-less steam engine designed to pump out water from mines.

1589 – English inventor William Lee creates the first knitting machine, apparently to please a woman he likes who is more interested in knitting than him! But Queen Elizabeth I refuses him a patent, fearing job losses. Lee moves to France, where he builds a thriving business making silk and woolen stockings.

1620 – English philosopher Francis Bacon describes modern experimental science in his Novum Organum, based on demonstration, observation, and experiment.

1669 – Nicolaus Steno, a Danish bishop, explains the formation of sedimentary rocks beneath the sea. He shows how the position of fossils in rock layers represents a chronology of life on Earth. His ideas lay the foundations of modern natural history.

1690 – French inventor Denis Papin builds a model of a piston steam engine.

DREBBEL

1644 – Florin Périer, Blaise Pascal's brother-in-law, shows that atmospheric pressure is lower up a mountain than at sea level. He proposes the Earth's atmosphere gradually thins out, eventually giving way to empty space.

1701 – English farmer Jethro Tull wins competitions with his horse-drawn seed drill that plants crops in rows, which are easier to weed and harvest. His invention ushers in an age of agricultural innovation.

1580 1590 1600 1610 1620 1630 1640 1650

1600 – William Gilbert, physician to Queen Elizabeth I, concludes the Earth is a magnet and coins the term "magnetic pole".

1628 – William Harvey, physician to James I and Charles I, establishes blood flows away from the heart in arteries and returns in veins.

Isaac Newton (1643–1727), a physicist from Lincolnshire, England, shines a beam of white light through a prism and discovers it is made up of all the colors in rainbow. Newton's book Principia (1687) describes gravity and three laws of motion that account for the movement of everything from an apple falling from a tree to the orbits of the planets around the Sun. He is considered by many to be the greatest and most influential scientist ever, and his discoveries help trigger an age of rational discovery known as "The Enlightenment".

1. If an object experiences no net force, then its velocity is constant.

3. When a body exerts a force on another body, the other body exerts an equal and opposite force on the first body.

TANGENT

1643 – Evangelista Torricelli, an Italian physicist, places a 3-foot mercury-filled tube, sealed at the top, open end downwards in a bowl of mercury. As atmospheric pressure changes, the mercury level moves up and down the tube. His barometer proves the existence of a vacuum.

1665 – Robert Hooke writes Micrographia, the Western world's first best-selling popular science book, after studying living things through a microscope. Fold-out plates reveal the intricate design of a fly's eyes, a flea's body, and a plant's "cells"—the basic units from which all living things are made.

n Gabriele Falloppio th dipped in salt as gainst syphilis during the first-ever clinical 00 men who use his adly sexually

1600 – Jakob Boehme, a German herbalist, suggests plants shaped like human body parts are signs from God they can cure diseases. His "doctrine of signatures" becomes popular throughout Europe.

1644 – Dutch chemist Jan Baptist van Helmont suggests there are insubstantial substances other than air, and calls them "gases".

1668 – John Mayow, a chemist and physician from Cornwall, England, argues particles in the air, "spiritus igneo-aereus," are responsible for combustion. He suggests such particles are essential to life and pass from the air through the lungs and into the blood.

1697 – German physician Georg Stahl proposes the existence of a fire-like element called phlogiston that is given off when things burn. The theory is widely accepted for at least 50 years until scientists discover that materials gain weight when they burn (oxidation).

1590 – Dutch lens grinders Hans and Zacharias Janssen are thought to have made the first compound microscope by placing two lenses in a tube.

1620 – English mathematician and inventor Edmund Gunter publishes the first logarithmic device, multiplying numbers using a single scale and a pair of dividers.

1637 – French mathematician René Descartes writes La Géométrie linking algebra and geometry with coordinates based on x and y axes. This visual system lays the foundations for calculus which shows how things move and change over time. Cartesian coordinates are used today for everything from statistics to mapmaking and satellite navigation.

1659 – Anglo-Irish chemist Robert Boyle constructs one of the first vacuum pumps. He puts a live lark in a jar and deprives it of air to observe the deadly effect of suffocation. From his experiments he also concludes light travels through a vacuum, although sound does not, and air is necessary for combustion.

1686 – The Royal Society is unable to publish Isaac Newton's Principia after exhausting funds producing a book about the history of fish. Newton's work is published with private funding donated by his friend Edmond Halley.

1710

1600 – Galileo Galilei, a Renaissance scholar from Pisa, Italy, discovers the principle of pendulums and the law on the behavior of moving bodies, contradicting the views of Aristotle that had been held for almost 2,000 years. Legend says he drops objects from the Tower of Pisa to prove that all objects fall at the same rate.

1632 – William Oughtred, a rector and mathematics teacher from Surrey, England, replaces Gunter's dividers with a pair of sliding rulers inscribed with sets of logarithmic scales. Slide rules remain popular until the invention of pocket calculators in the 1970s.

1656 – Christiaan Huygens invents the pendulum mechanism, allowing the creation of clocks that are accurate to within 10 seconds a day.

1662 – Robert Boyle proposes a universal law, subsequently called Boyle's Law, which states if the volume of a gas halves, its pressure will double—and vice versa—provided its temperature is constant. Boyle's book, The Sceptical Chymist, helps establish chemistry as a branch of science.

1678 – Robert Hooke outlines the principles of elasticity. Hooke's Law states that an extension of a spring is in direct proportion to the load applied to it—until it reaches its "elastic limit."

$$\int f(x)dx = g(x) + c$$

1675 – German mathematician Gottfried Leibniz develops calculus independently of Isaac Newton. His system of notation is eventually adopted worldwide.

1714 – Daniel Fah invents a scale me temperature in wh water freezes at 32 and boils at 212°F.

1614 – Scottish mathematician John Napier shows how to simplify calculations by using logarithms. His look-up tables—which are adopted by engineers, scientists, and navigators—pave the way for the development of the slide rule. He also invents a set of rods marked with digits so that, by arranging them side by side in an appropriate order, complex multiplications can be performed.

1637 – Pierre de Fermat, an amateur French mathematician, scribbles in the margin of a copy of Diophantus's Arithmetica that he has a proof that the equation $x^n + y^n = z^n$ has no solution for $n > 2$, but he fails to write it down! Fermat's Last Theorem isn't finally proven for another 358 years.

$$a^n + b^n = c^n$$

1645 – French mathematician Blaise Pascal invents a rudimentary mechanical calculator to help his father, a tax collector, do his sums.

1654 – French lawyer Pierre de Fermat and Blaise Pascal lay the foundations of probability theory, proving why rolling at least one six in four throws of a die is more probable than rolling at least one double-six in 24 throws of two dice.

1665 – Pascal's Treatise on Arithmetical Triangles is published posthumously. It shows how a sequence of numbers can be organized in a triangle (now known as Pascal's triangle) to solve problems in probability theory.

Triangle Arithmétique.

1	1	1	1	1	1	1	1
1	2	3	4	5	6	7	8
1	3	6	10	15	21	28	
1	4	10	20	35	56		
1	5	15	35	70	126		
1	6	21	56				
1	7	28					
1	8						

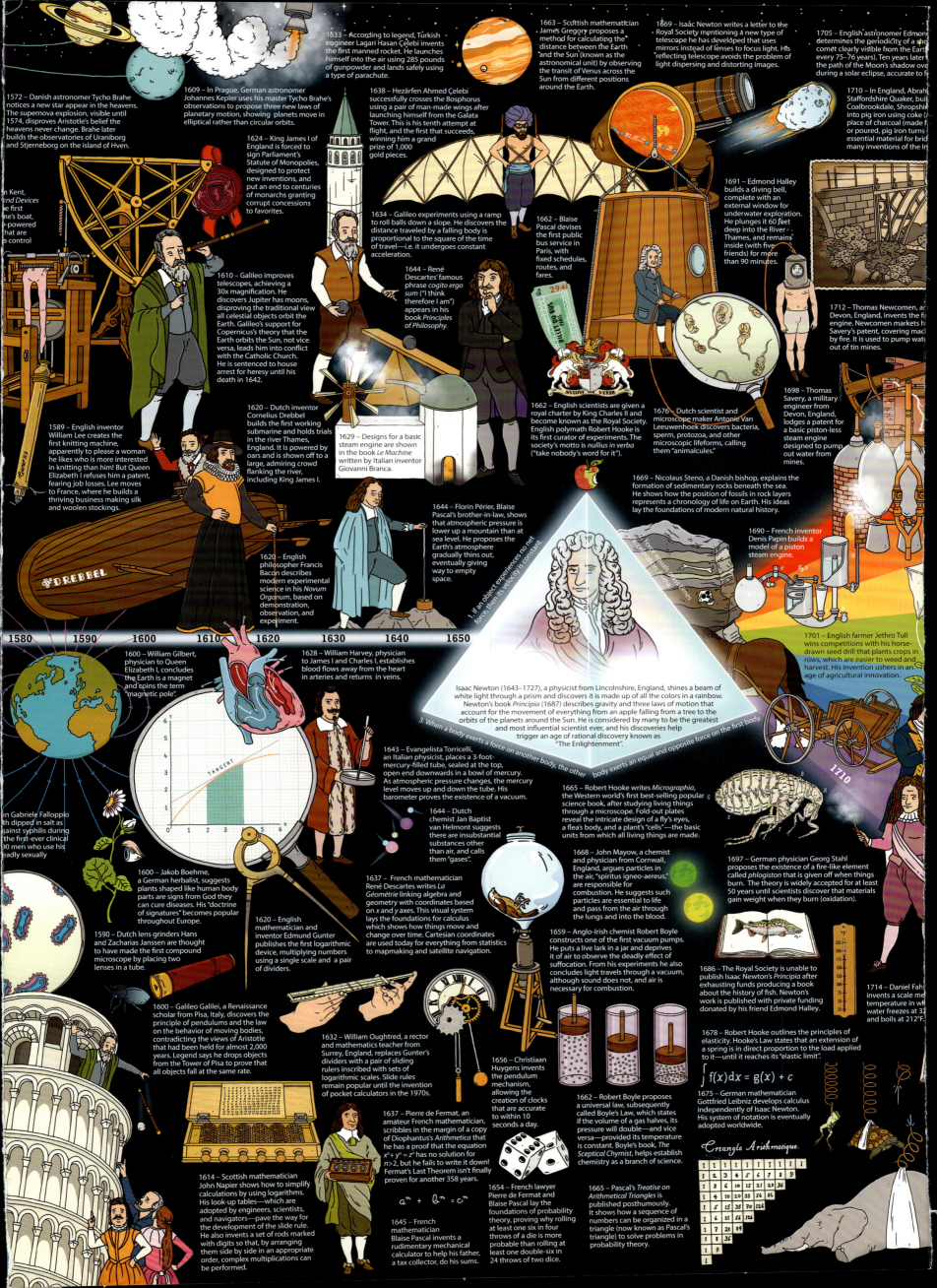

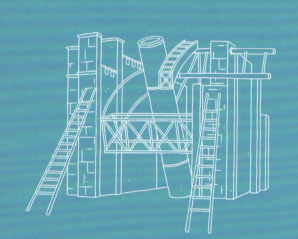

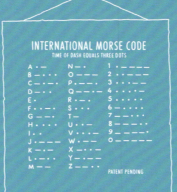

INTERNATIONAL MORSE CODE
TIME OF DASH EQUALS THREE DOTS

A ·—	N —·	1 ·————
B —···	O ———	2 ··———
C —·—·	P ·——·	3 ···——
D —··	Q ——·—	4 ····—
E ·	R ·—·	5 ·····
F ··—·	S ···	6 —····
G ——·	T —	7 ——···
H ····	U ··—	8 ———··
I ··	V ···—	9 ————·
J ·———	W ·——	0 —————
K —·—	X —··—	
L ·—··	Y —·——	
M ——	Z ——··	PATENT PENDING

Edmund Halley short-period [comet] (it returns near the Earth every 76 years) ... predicts the [return] ... four minutes.

[Abraham] Darby I, [founds] a new blast furnace at [Coalbrookdale], that can turn iron ore [into a refined form of charred coal) from wood). When melted [it turns] into cast iron, an [essential for forges], steam engines, and [the] Industrial Revolution.

1735 – British meteorologist George Hadley proposes that trade winds blow eastwards when moving away from the equator and westwards when moving toward it.

1738 – Swiss mathematician and physicist Daniel Bernoulli writes *Hydrodynamica* outlining his kinetic theory of gases, stating how pressure is always reduced when velocity increases, such as when air passes over an aircraft wing.

[An] ironmonger from [the first] practical steam [engine]. His engine under [mines powered]

1759 – English civil and mechanical engineer John Smeaton rediscovers how to make cement, a process forgotten in the West since the collapse of the Roman Empire. His quick-setting limestone-and-clay concrete is used to build the foundations of the Eddystone Lighthouse.

1738 – French clockwork engineer Jacques de Vaucanson makes ingenious automatons, including androids that can serve dinner and a flute player with 12 songs. His masterpiece *The Digesting Duck* has 400 moving parts in each wing and can drink, digest, and excrete.

1740 – British quaker Benjamin Huntsman casts steel in clay ingots or "crucibles." Cast steel can be forged into products such as springs.

1733 – John Kay invents the flying shuttle, making mass production of broadcloth textiles more efficient.

1753 – Swedish botanist Carolus Linnaeus introduces binomial nomenclature (for example, *Homo sapiens*), first used in his *Species Plantarum*.

1727 – In *Vegetable Staticks*, English botanist Stephen Hales describes the transpiration process in plants—as water evaporates out of a plant's leaves, water is absorbed through its roots.

1730s – Charles "Turnip" Townshend popularizes the practice of crop rotation to help maintain soil fertility.

1734 – English mathematician John Hadley makes a reflecting octant (originally designed by Isaac Newton) —a device for measuring the angle of the Sun and stars, allowing accurate time-keeping and navigation at sea.

1738 – Abraham de Moivre's second edition of *The Doctrine of Chances* describes a pattern of probability now called "normal distribution," represented graphically by a bell curve.

1732 – Laura Bassi, a home-educated Italian physicist, is the first woman to be a professor at a European university. She introduces Newtonian physics to Italy at the University of Bologna.

1742 – Swedish astronomer Anders Celsius makes a thermometer with water freezing at 100°C and boiling at 0°C. His centigrade scale is reversed after his death.

1761 & 1769 – international scientists collaborate on a series of expeditions to observe the transit of Venus to calculate the distance of the Sun from the Earth. The explorers include Captain James Cook who, after observing the transit from Tahiti, maps the coasts of New Zealand and Australia. Results show the distance to be 93 million miles.

1750 – French astronomer Nicolas de Lacaille sails to the southern oceans and catalogs more than 10,000 stars, the first detailed mapping of the heavens of the southern hemisphere.

1769 – Nicolas-Joseph Cugnot builds a "steam wagon," a precursor to the first automobile.

1769 – Scottish engineer James Watt builds steam engines with a separate chamber as a condenser. His double-action engine lets in steam at both ends of the cylinder and is powerful enough to drive machinery and mills.

1775 – Scotsman Alexander Cummings patents a flushing toilet, complete with S-bend to block bad smells.

1769 – English barber Richard Arkwright invents a water-powered spinning frame, revolutionizing the making of cloth from cotton.

1764 – James Hargreaves invents a multi-spool spinning frame. His "Spinning Jenny" needs fewer workers to produce yarn, beginning the process of mass production of cotton products.

1761 – Italian anatomist Giovanni Morgagni publishes a treatise based on dissections of 646 people who had died of various diseases. His work establishes pathology as a distinct science.

1754 – Scottish chemist Joseph Black measures the weight of materials before and after chemical reactions and concludes that carbon dioxide (called "fixed air") is given off when limestone is heated. He discovers the same gas is emitted by animals and forms part of the atmosphere. He proves air is not an element, but a mixture of gases.

1752 – American genius Benjamin Franklin describes flying a kite in a thunderstorm to demonstrate it is an electrical phenomena. His work contributes to the invention of lightning conductors.

1745 – A foil-lined glass jar that stores static electricity is invented independently by two scientists working in the Dutch city of Leyden. Ewald Georg von Kleist's and Pieter van Musschenbroek's Leyden jars allow practical experiments with electricity. It becomes fashionable to give electric shocks to servants and children as a form of punishment.

1747 – Scottish physician James Lind finds a treatment for scurvy by giving sailors citrus fruit.

1759 – English watchmaker John Harrison invents a marine chronometer that measures time at sea accurately, allowing sailors to calculate their longitude by comparing their homeport time (shown by the chronometer) with the local time (shown by the Sun). It takes Harrison 31 years to perfect.

1770 – Swiss mathematician Leonhard Euler transforms mathematics by introducing the concept of a function f(x) and notation such as Σ for summation and *i* for the imaginary unit.

1776 – Scotsman Adam Smith publishes *An Inquiry into the Nature and Causes of the Wealth of Nations*, considered to be the first work of the branch of science now called economics.

1781 – French astronomer Charles Messier's astronomical catalog lists 103 deep space objects, including comets, nebulae, and galaxies.

1781 – German-born British astronomer William Herschel discovers a planet. Initially it is called the "Georgian star" in honor of King George III, but is later renamed Uranus.

1783 – French engineers Joseph-Michel and Jacques-Étienne Montgolfier build a hot-air balloon carrying a sheep, a duck, and a rooster to see if they can survive at high altitude. The flight reaches 1,500 feet and lasts 8 minutes.

1787 – American inventor John Fitch and clockmaker Henry Voigt make the first steamboat using oars powered by a steam engine.

1791 – John Barber receives British patent no. 1833 for his turbine in *A Method of Rising Inflammable Air for the Purposes of Procuring Motion, and Facilitating Metallurgical Operations.*

1779 – Samuel Crompton invents the spinning mule, allowing just one operator to supervise the spinning of 1,000 reels of fine yarn. The invention helps make Britain the world leader in fabric production.

1785 – Joseph Bramah invents a hydraulic pump to draw beer up from a tavern cellar. He later invents a press for shaping metal.

BRAMAH

1779 – Dutch botanist Jan Ingenhousz discovers the necessities for plant photosynthesis: sunlight, water, and carbon dioxide. He shows the process gives off oxygen.

1788 – Scottish naturalist James Hutton suggests there are three types of rock: igneous, sedimentary, and metamorphic. He is considered the father of geology.

1780 – Italian scientist Luigi Galvani notices the legs of a dead frog twitch when touched by an iron wire. He concludes a form of "animal electricity" is responsible for making muscles move.

1783 – Henry Cavendish discovers that water is made of hydrogen and oxygen.

1793 – German naturalist Christian Sprengel discovers sexual reproduction in plants. Scientists ridicule Sprengel's theory.

1775 – British scientist John Mervin Nooth invents a machine that mixes sulfuric acid and soda lime to add bubbles to water. Joseph Priestley claims this artificially carbonated water has the medicinal qualities of natural springs.

1774 – Joseph Priestley, an English chemist, focuses the Sun's rays on mercuric oxide and discovers a gas—later called oxygen—which he calls "dephlogisticated air".

1794 – French nobleman and chemist Antoine Lavoisier is executed by revolutionaries on trumped-up charges. It ends the life of a remarkable scientist who laid the foundations for modern chemistry, named oxygen and hydrogen, and wrote the first detailed list of elements.

1785 – French physicist Charles-Augustin de Coulomb uses a torsion balance to study the interaction of charged particles. He discovers there is an inverse relationship between the strength of force between two electric charges and the square of their distance—Coulomb's law.

1785 – English potter Josiah Wedgwood (grandfather of Charles Darwin) invents the pyrometer, a gauge for measuring the temperature of kilns using clay blocks that shrink as they get hotter.

1787 – The theodolite, an instrument for measuring angles, is perfected by scientific toolmaker Jesse Ramsden from Yorkshire, England. It is first used to calculate distances between observatories in Greenwich, in London, and Paris for astronomical calculations, but eventually helps create the Ordnance Survey of Great Britain.

1796 – French astronomer Pierre-Simon Laplace proposes that the planets in our solar system originally formed from a nebulous ring of material that orbited the Sun. He also suggests that stars may sometimes collapse through intense gravity to form what we now call black holes.

1804 – Frenchman Joseph Gay-Lussac discovers that the composition of the air does not change with increasing altitude (decreasing pressure).

1801 – Richard Trevithick, a mining engineer from Cornwall, England, builds the first high-pressure steam engine. His *Puffing Devil* road-locomotive carries several men from Camborne in Cornwall to the nearby village of Beacon.

1804 – Joseph Marie Jacquard perfects the Jacquard Loom which uses punched cards to weave complex designs. It later inspires computer design.

1807 – German inventor Friedrich Winzer patents gas lighting first used in London.

1794 – American inventor Eli Whitney patents the cotton gin, automating the separation of cotton seed from short-staple cotton fiber.

1791 – A grand Ordnance Survey project maps Great Britain from a 5-mile baseline on Hounslow Heath in London.

HOUNSLOW HEATH

1804 – Swiss botanist Nicolas-Théodore de Saussure reveals the role of chlorophyll in photosynthesis.

1797 – English scientist Henry Cavendish measures the force of gravity between large globes. From this he estimates the Earth's density is 5.45 times greater than water.

1805 – Friedrich Sertürner makes a painkiller from poppy juice. He names the drug morphine after Morpheus, the Greek god of sleep.

1796 – Edward Jenner, a doctor from Gloucestershire, England, vaccinates both arms of eight-year-old James Phipps with blister fluid from a milkmaid with cowpox. Jenner infects the boy with smallpox but he shows no signs of infection.

1804 – Japanese surgeon Seishu Hanaoka uses plant extracts atropine and scopolamine as the first modern general anesthetic. Similar chemicals are used in anesthetics today.

1800 – William Herschel passes sunlight through a prism and finds the temperature beyond the red of the visible spectrum is higher than the temperature in the room. He concludes there is an invisible form of light, now known as infrared.

INFRARED

VISIBLE SPECTRUM

1800 – Italian physicist Alessandro Volta invents a battery producing a steady current in a circuit. His *voltaic pile* is a stack of disks of brine-soaked paper, zinc, and copper.

1803 – English teacher John Dalton proposes that an element is a substance that cannot be broken down into compounds are atoms of two or more elements. He devises symbols for atoms of 36 different elements, their atomic weights compared with hydrogen.

ELEMENTS			
⊙ Hydrogen	1	Ⓢ Strontian	46
⊘ Azote	5	Ⓑ Barytes	68
● Carbon	5	Ⓘ Iron	50
⊖ Oxygen	7	Ⓩ Zinc	56
⊕ Phosphorus	9	Ⓒ Copper	56
⊕ Sulpur	13	Ⓛ Lead	90

LOW PRESSURE

WATER EVAPORATES

WATER TRANSPORTED

WATER ABSORBED

OXYGEN

CARBON DIOXIDE

1730   1740   1750   1760   1770   1780   1790   1800

£20 Twenty Pounds Bank of England

Σ

…turn's…

…Clausius restates Carnot's … in mathematics, calling it … constantly moving from a …

…m entropy

…ent receives … first pedal … cranks …

1877 – Austrian physicist Ernst Mach describes the shock wave that is generated when objects move at supersonic speeds.

1877 – Enrico Forlanini, an Italian engineer, makes the world's first successful helicopter. The steam-powered, unmanned vehicle rises by 43 feet and stays up for 20 seconds after lifting off in a Milan park.

1893 – German aviator Otto Lilienthal pioneers heavier-than-air flight with a series of jumps using a hang glider. He travels over 820 feet through the air. After a later jump goes wrong, his dying words are "small sacrifices must be made...".

TROPOSPHERE

MESOSPHERE

IONOSPHERE

STRATOSPHERE

1902 – The ionosphere is discovered as a result of early radio transmissions unexpectedly colliding with charged particles produced by the Sun's radiation and bouncing back to Earth. This makes it possible to send shortwave radio messages around the world.

WHITE DWARF

RED GIANT

1910 – Danish astronomer Ejnar Hertzsprung and American Henry Russell categorize stars into different types depending on their luminosity, e.g. white dwarfs and red giants.

1919 – British astrophysicist Arthur Eddington travels to Principe, an island off West Africa, and observes starlight bending around the Sun during a solar eclipse, proving Einstein's General Theory of Relativity.

1873 – C. L. Scholes invents the typewriter with a QWERTY keyboard.

1876 – Inventor Alexander Graham Bell patents a working telephone. His system converts sound into electrical signals and back again. Five years later he invents the first metal detector.

1884 – Lewis Waterman makes the fountain pen a mass-market product.

1895 – The Lumière brothers project the first motion pictures.

1884 – Sir Charles Parsons builds a steam turbine and a turbine-powered boat, *Turbinia* (first demonstrated in 1897).

1903 – Bicycle-shop owners Orville and Wilbur Wright make the first powered, heavier-than-air human flight at Kitty Hawk, North Carolina, in the *Flyer*—a home-built aircraft with a light aluminum internal-combustion engine built by Charlie Taylor.

1909 – French headlight maker and aviator Louis Blériot wins a $4,870 prize from the *Daily Mail* newspaper for being the first person to cross the English Channel in an airplane. The journey from Calais to Dover takes 36 minutes and 30 seconds.

1914 – The last passenger pigeon dies in America, showing how easily humans can cause the extinction of a once prolific species.

1901 – Italian Guglielmo Marconi claims to make the first successful radio transmission across the Atlantic using a 490-foot kite-supported antenna.

1876 – Nikolaus Otto's stationary internal-combustion engine uses a crankshaft and a four-stroke cycle to generate circular motion. Ten years later, Karl Benz makes the world's first three-wheeled motorwagon, while Gottlieb Daimler builds the first four-wheeled car.

1868 – J. P. Knight invents the first traffic lights, installed at a junction in Westminster, London, which then explode a month later.

1908 – Henry Ford's Model T Ford rolls off the production line—the world's first affordable car.

1918 – HMS *Argus* becomes the world's first fully operational aircraft carrier with a full-length flight deck.

…chemist Alfred Nobel patents … nitroglycerine called dynamite … onated with a gunpowder fuse … ia a cable. His fortune is used … ience, literature, and peace.

1877 – Self-educated American Thomas Edison invents a range of devices including the phonograph, the first machine able to record and play back sound, which uses a tinfoil cylinder and stylus. His most famous achievement is inventing an incandescent light bulb that actually works!

1888 – Scotsman John Dunlop invents the pneumatic tire for his son's tricycle.

1889 – Gustave Eiffel, a French engineer, builds an iron lattice tower for the Universal Exposition in Paris.

1893 – American engineer George Ferris builds the first Ferris wheel in Chicago, in a bid to "out-Eiffel Eiffel".

1897 – Rudolf Diesel invents a highly efficient type of combustion engine, which initially runs on peanut oil.

1901 – British engineer Hubert Booth invents the powered vacuum cleaner.

1906 – American inventor Lee de Forest makes a primitive electronic amplifier called an Audion. Derivatives (called triodes) help make long-distance radio and telephony possible.

1907 – Belgian inventor Leo Baekeland unveils a new type of plastic which is easy to shape and highly durable. He calls it Bakelite.

1914 – A 48-mile canal is completed in Panama linking the Atlantic and Pacific oceans. It takes 33 years to complete. Disease and accidents affect an estimated 22,000 workers.

PANAMA CANAL

1869 - The Governor of New York, John Thompson Hoffman, signs the Act of Incorporation officially creating the American Museum of Natural History on April 6.

1882 – Thomas Edison opens the first urban electricity system, serving 508 customers with 10,164 lamps in New York by 1884.

1887 – Emile Berliner invents the gramophone, using disks instead of cylinders.

1901 – Welsh engineer Edgar Purnell Hooley patents Tarmac after noticing someone attempt to clear up a barrel of spilt tar by pouring gravel over it.

1909 – German scientists Fritz Haber and Carl Bosch pioneer an industrial process to make ammonia, used for the production of fertilizers and artificial explosives.

1911 – General Electric unveils the first domestic refrigerator. Mass production begins in 1927.

1914 – British Prime Minister David Lloyd George imports 5,000 Fordson tractors from the United States in a bid to beat starvation from a German U-boat blockade. It leads to the mechanization of farming in the UK.

1920s – Al… promotes … agriculture … to India—he … "organic farr…

1878 – Biologist Alfred Russel Wallace warns against deforestation, invasive species, soil erosion, and habitat destruction as a result of human activities.

1887 – Fed up with servants breaking plates, Josephine Cochrane designs the first automatic dishwasher and starts what will become the KitchenAid company.

1897 – German chemist Eduard Buchner discovers that glucose ferments using only extracts of yeast. He realizes enzymes cause the chemical reactions vital for life.

1869 – British biologist and ardent Darwin supporter Thomas Huxley uses the word "agnostic" to describe the opinion that the existence of God cannot be known.

1880s – Steam tractors begin to be used on farms throughout North America for plowing, threshing, and pulling agricultural loads. Road-builders use adapted models as steamrollers.

PANGAEA

1912 – Alfred Wegener proposes the world's continents were once joined in a giant supercontinent, Pangaea (Greek for "all the Earth"). His theory is not widely accepted until the 1960s.

1916 – Californian Benjamin Holt invents the first crawler-type tread tractor in 1904. In WWI his designs haul artillery, and lead to the development of tanks in warfare.

…endel, an Austrian monk, … pea plants and discovers … smooth and wrinkled peas … characteristics are passed … 3:1 rather than 1:1.

1868 – Joseph Lister pioneers antiseptic surgery with operations conducted in germ-free environments, finally opening up the abdomen, thorax, and cranium to the surgeon's scalpel.

1870 – American John Hyatt invents celluloid, a polymer made of nitrocellulose and camphor. Uses include false teeth and photographic film.

1878 – German biologist Walther Flemming describes the separation and duplication of cellular threads (later called chromosomes) which he calls *mitosis*.

PROPHASE

METAPHASE

ANAPHASE

TELOPHASE

1888 – Francis Galton develops fingerprinting for use in criminal investigation and identification, since the probability of two people having identical prints is extremely remote.

1881 – American engineer James Bonsack patents a machine that may have led to more deaths than any other: an automatic cigarette-rolling machine that can manufacture 200 cigarettes a minute.

1897 – German chemist Felix Hoffman makes the first medically useful form of aspirin.

1901 – Austrian biologist Karl Landsteiner discovers there are four blood groups, each one containing different chemicals called antigens responsible for immune response.

A ANTIGEN

B ANTIGEN

BLOOD TYPE A

BLOOD TYPE B

BLOOD TYPE AB UNIVERSAL RECIPIENT

BLOOD TYPE O UNIVERSAL DONOR

1905 – German bacteriologist Robert Koch receives the Nobel Prize in Medicine for identifying bacteria as disease-causing agents.

INCREASING ALKALINITY

NEUTRAL

INCREASING ACIDITY

1911 – After studies on a mutant white-eyed variety of fruit fly (*Drosophila*), American geneticist Thomas Hunt Morgan establishes genes are attached to chromosomes, which explains how specific traits are inherited.

1909 – German scientist Korbinian Brodmann identifies 52 areas of the brain, each with a different function.

1909 – Danish chemist Søren Sørensen devises a logarithmic scale introducing the concept of pH. Solutions with a pH less than 7 are acidic, those greater are basic, or alkaline.

1914 – X-rays are used to determine the structure of table salt and diamond. The technique is later refined and becomes known as X-ray crystallography and allows the observation of matter at an atomic scale.

THE PERIODIC TABLE ~ Dmitri Mendeleev 1869

1869 – Russian chemist Dmitri Mendeleev finds a pattern linking the different chemical elements. His periodic table, grouping elements with similar properties, becomes standard.

1884 – Swedish chemist Svante Arrhenius defines an acid solution as having excess hydrogen ions and an alkali as having excess hydroxide ions. He proposes an excess of these charged particles is responsible for corrosion by acids and alkalis.

1903 – Polish scientist Marie Curie receives the Nobel Prize in Physics, shared with French collaborator Henri Becquerel and her husband Pierre. In 1911 she also wins the Nobel Prize in Chemistry for her discovery of the elements polonium and radium.

1909 – Hans Geiger and Ernest Marsden, working under Ernest Rutherford, fire a stream of positively charged alpha particles through a sheet of gold foil in a vacuum. Most of the alpha particles pass through, but some bounce back. Rutherford deduces atoms contain a tiny but highly dense nucleus.

1913 – Danish physicist Niels Bohr says electrons orbit an atom's nucleus in a series of fixed shells. They gain or lose energy only when they jump from one orbit to another.

1906 – British physicist Joseph Thomson wins the Nobel Prize in Physics for discovering electrons, the negatively charged components of atoms.

1900 – French physicist Paul Villard discovers high-frequency electromagnetic rays coming from radium. They are named "gamma" rays by Ernest Rutherford.

1917 – Ernest Rutherford "splits the atom" using nitrogen and a beam of alpha particles. In the process he discovers the proton.

1918 – German engineer Arthur Scherbius invents a cipher machine using a series of rotating wired wheels. Used by Nazis in WWII, it becomes known as the Enigma machine.

GAMMA

X RAY

ULTRAVIOLET

VISIBLE

INFRARED

MICROWAVES

RADIO WAVES

1880s – English electrical engineer John Ambrose Fleming invents the vacuum tube and diode (1904) and develops left- and right-hand rules to explain electrical motors and generators.

1895 – German physicist Wilhelm Röntgen publishes a paper entitled *On a New Kind of Rays* in which he describes his discovery of X-rays.

1893 – German physicist Victor Schumann uses a fluorite prism and lens to detect extreme ultraviolet radiation.

1899 – New Zealand-born British physicist Ernest Rutherford proves radioactive decay changes one substance into another. He identifies two types of atomic radiation: heavy "alpha" particles that travel short distances and cannot penetrate paper; and lighter "beta" particles that travel farther.

1911 – Dutch physicist Heike Kamerlingh Onnes discovers superconductivity—when some substances are cooled close to absolute zero, they lose all electrical resistance.

…James Clerk Maxwell writes … of mathematical equations … electromagnetic forces … e same speed as light … miles per second). His … proposes the existence … trum of electromagnetic … n at different wavelengths … isible light.

1880 – A single national time—Greenwich Mean Time—is made law in Britain to help co-ordinate railroad schedules. Standard time is adopted across the U.S. and Canada three years later.

1888 – German physicist Heinrich Hertz discovers radio waves and shows they reflect off solid objects in the same way as light, confirming Maxwell's theory that light is a form of electromagnetic radiation. His discovery eventually leads to the development of RAdio Detection And Ranging (RADAR), as radio waves reflect off electrically conductive objects such as metallic ships and planes.

1900 – German physicist Max Planck proposes that electromagnetic radiation is transmitted in packets of energy called "quanta." The idea is later developed into "quantum" theory.

$E = mc^2$

1905 – German physicist Albert Einstein publishes a paper detailing the Special Theory of Relativity in which he proposes that Isaac Newton's laws of motion break down as objects approach the speed of light. His theory implies that atoms contain vast quantities of energy according to the equation: E (energy) = m (mass) times c (the speed of light) squared, or $E = mc^2$.

1916 – Einstein publishes his *General Theory of Relativity* in which he demonstrates how gravitational fields distort time and space. His theory leads to the idea that the Universe contains black holes, vortices of immense gravitation from which even light cannot escape.

1870 1880 1890 1900 1910 1920

1929 – American astronomers Edwin Hubble and Vesto Slipher take measurements showing that all observable galaxies are spreading outwards. Their theory provides the first evidence for the idea the Universe began 13.7 billion years ago with the "Big Bang".

1939 – Robert Oppenheimer and George Volkoff propose black holes are formed by the collapse of neutron stars about three times more massive than the Sun.

1957 – On October 4, the USSR launches Sputnik the first artificial satellite. Sputnik 2 launches a month later and carries the first living creature into space, Laika the dog, triggering a space race with the USA.

1962 – The first telecoms satellite, Telstar 1, allows 60 simultaneous transatlantic phone calls and the first satellite TV broadcasts.

1966 – Wernher von Braun masterminds development of the Saturn V, rocket which powers the Apollo Moon missions.

1926 – American scientist Robert Goddard builds the world's first liquid-fuelled rocket. Over the next 15 years, he launches 34 rockets, pioneering multistage rocket design, gyroscopes and steerable thrust.

1944 – V1 flying bombs, Doodlebugs, are fired at the people of London by Nazi Germany, the first use of long-range missiles.

1949 – The first commercial jet, the de Havilland DH 106 Comet, makes its maiden flight but is redesigned after several fatal crashes.

1961 – U.S. President John F. Kennedy sets a national goal of "landing a man on the Moon and returning him safely to Earth" before the end of the decade.

1969 – On July 20, at 20:18 GMT, Neil Armstrong and Buzz Aldrin become the first people to land on the Moon. Armstrong steps on the surface six hours later.

1937 – German passenger airship LZ 129 Hindenburg catches fire and is destroyed in just under 40 seconds, killing 36 people, while landing in New Jersey.

1939 – German engineer Hans von Ohain builds the first jet plane, the Heinkel He 178. Its maiden flight is held in great secrecy on the eve of WWII and reaches speeds of up to 372 mph.

1961 – Soviet Yuri Gagarin is the first human to journey into space.

1922 – The BBC is founded to broadcast experimental radio services.

1930 – British engineer Frank Whittle patents the jet engine.

1959 – The first photocopier not to use wet chemicals is marketed by Haloid Xerox.

HALOID XEROX ROCHESTER, N.Y.

1964 – The first Bullet Train enters service in Japan between Tokyo and Osaka with a top speed of 130.5 mph.

1925 – Scottish engineer John Logie Baird makes the first public TV demonstrations at Selfridges store in London. America's first TV station W2XB begins broadcasting three years later.

BAIRD TELEVISION

1938 – László Bíró from Hungary patents the design for the modern ballpoint pen.

1938 – Mallard, an A4 steam engine designed by Scottish engineer Sir Nigel Gresley, sets the world speed record for a steam locomotive at 125.88 mph.

1947 – Americans John Bardeen, William Shockley, and Walter Brattain place a germanium crystal on a conducting base, creating the transistor for switching and amplifying electronic signals.

1958 & 1959 – American engineers Jack Kilby and Robert Noyce design the first integrated circuits (microchip). Noyce's design allows a circuit to fit on a single silicon chip.

1964 – The Ford Motor Company launches the Ford Mustang—the world's first affordable mass-market sports car

1970 – The first electronic digital wristwatch is made by John Bergey of Pulsar, inspired by the 1968 sci-fi film 2001: A Space Odyssey.

1948 – American scientist Edwin Land invents the Polaroid instant camera, allowing photos to be taken and developed in less than a minute.

1924 – The Toyoda Automatic Loom, Type G, is the first automatic high-speed loom able to change shuttles without stopping, multiplying productivity by 20 times. Profits launch the Toyota Motor Company.

TOYODA

1935 – Wallace Carothers of the DuPont chemical company invents a new artificial plastic fiber. Nylon stockings become popular during WWII when Asian silk becomes scarce.

1936 – Frank Hornby, English toymaker and inventor dies.

DINKY TOYS

1926 – American Charles Strite invents the pop-up toaster.

1934 – American Laurens Hammond invents an electric organ.

1928 – American Colonel Jacob Schick invents the electric razor.

1936 – Texan musician George Beauchamp invents the electric guitar.

1941 – Swiss engineer George de Mestral sees burrs attached to his dog after a walk in the Alps and invents Velcro.

1938 – Hydroponics allows farmers to grow plants in a solution of liquid nutrients rather than soil.

ARCO IDAHO — FIRST CITY IN THE WORLD TO BE LIT BY ATOMIC POWER — ELEVATION 5320

1959 – The world's first hovercraft, the SR-N1, invented by Christopher Cockerell, crosses the English Channel.

1965 – Gordon Moore, cofounder of Intel, predicts the number of transistors on a microchip will double about every two years. Moore's Law is expected to hold until at least 2020.

1926 – Russian scientist Vladimir Vernadsky founds the discipline of Earth science combining geology, history, and biology in his book The Biosphere.

CHARLES RICHTER SCALE

D.D.T

1951 – Electricity from an atomic power station, the National Reactor Testing Station at Arco, Idaho, is produced for the first time.

1961 – The World Wildlife Fund is founded.

WWF — WORLD WILDLIFE FUND

1962 – American marine biologist Rachel Carson writes Silent Spring on the damaging effects of synthetic pesticides such as DDT on nature, especially birds. She stimulates a new environmental awareness in the West.

1935 – Charles Richter devises a scale to measure earthquakes. Each step represents a more than 30-fold increase in the amount of energy released.

1939 – Paul Müller discovers the potential of DDT, first synthesized in 1874, as a pesticide. It is later banned for causing massive ecological damage.

1943 – Willem Kolff, a Dutch physician, develops the first artificial kidney, a dialysis machine, using sausage skins.

1955 – American scientist Charles Keeling measures the amount of carbon dioxide in the air. His measurements over the next 40 years show dramatic rises, widely attributed to human activities.

1935 – English botanist Arthur Tansley sets out the idea of an ecosystem with the Sun's power cascading through a food web.

1950 – Australian scientists release the lethal virus myxomatosis into the wild to control huge rabbit populations. It kills more than 500 million rabbits in just two years.

1960 – U.S. Navy officer Harry Hess provides a mechanism for Wegener's theories on moving continents, following the 1953 discovery of the Mid-Atlantic Ridge. He says oceanic crust is formed by magma rising in mid-ocean trenches, causing older sea floor to spread outward.

1951 – English-born physician John Wild pioneers the use of ultrasound for imaging unborn babies and diagnosing cancer.

1953 – Scientists James Watson and Francis Crick, aided by X-ray crystallography from Rosalind Franklin, announce in Nature magazine their discovery of the double helix structure of DNA. Their research shows how genes pass from one generation to the next.

1954 – American surgeon Joseph Murray performs the world's first successful organ transplant, taking a kidney from Ronald Herrick to save the life of his twin, Richard.

1928 – Scottish bacteriologist Alexander Fleming goes on holiday, leaving his laboratory at St. Mary's Hospital, London, without properly washing his petri dishes. On return he discovers one with a curious transparent ring, caused by fungal mold that has killed surrounding bacteria. Fleming identifies the fungus as Penicillium and names the antibacterial chemical it produces "penicillin".

ca. 1930 – Thomas Midgley uses artificially synthesized chlorofluorocarbons (CFCs) as unreactive, low-cost aerosol and refrigerant.

PENICILLIN

1967 – South African surgeon Christian Barnard and his team perform the first heart transplant. The patient, Louis Washkansky, a grocer from Cape Town, dies 18 days later.

1969 – British chemist Dorothy Hodgkin advances the techniques of X-ray crystallography to identify the atomic structures for a range of important biomolecules, including insulin, cholesterol, penicillin, and vitamin B_{12}.

1940 – Building on Alexander Fleming's work on penicillin, Australian pathologist Howard Florey and German biochemist Ernst Chain turn penicillin into a treatment curing many human diseases.

KRYLON

1945 – The Gadget is detonated in the Nevada desert. It contains just 22 pounds of radioactive material but releases energy equivalent to 22,045 tons of TNT. Weeks later U.S. planes drop two atom bombs on Japan.

1952 – American scientists Harold Urey and Stanley Miller make amino acids, the building blocks of life, out of simple chemicals. Their research stimulates debate about how life may have begun 4 billion years ago.

1958 – The first implantable heart pacemaker is made by Swedes Rune Elmqvist and Åke Senning.

1959 – English engineer Francis Bacon builds the first modern hydrogen-oxygen fuel cell. They are used for the Apollo space missions.

1932 – James Chadwick discovers the neutron, leading to its use to split the atom in bombs and power stations.

1927 – Physicists agree on the Copenhagen interpretation, a key tenet of quantum mechanics, stating subatomic systems have no defined state until observed, after which it is fixed. The concept is later explained by Erwin Schrödinger in 1935 saying a cat trapped in a box can be considered both alive and dead at the same time.

1933 – Hungarian physicist Leo Szilard suggests enough neutrons can split from radioactive material to split further atoms continually in a nuclear chain reaction, creating an almost limitless supply of energy. Nine years later, Enrico Fermi creates the first nuclear fission chain reaction.

1948 – Austrian engineer Curt Herzstark perfects the Curta, a pocket mechanical calculator he designed in a Nazi concentration camp.

1965 – Richard Feynman uses a series of diagrams to show how light (photons) and electricity (electrons) interact in his theory of Quantum Electrodynamics (QED).

1960 – American physicist Theodore Maiman builds the world's first LASER (Light Amplification by the Stimulated Emission of Radiation) using a synthetic ruby crystal.

ELECTRODE — WATER VAPOR — COOLED WATER — NASA

1928 – British physicist Paul Dirac details the math behind quantum mechanics (known as the Dirac equation) and proposes the existence of antimatter particles sharing the same mass and quantum spin as matter particles but with opposite charge. Direct evidence of the existence of antimatter particles is discovered four years later by American physicist Carl Anderson.

$$\left(\beta mc^2 + \sum_{n=1}^{3} \alpha_n p_n c \right) \psi(x,t) = i\hbar \frac{\partial \psi(x,t)}{\partial t}$$

1936 – Alan Turing, a British mathematician, imagines a computing machine that follows a set of rules governing the way it reads, writes, and erases symbols on an infinite tape. It only ever exists as pencil notes but has a huge influence on modern computing.

1944 – British engineer Tommy Flowers develops Colossus, the first fixed-program digital computer, used to aid British codebreakers in WWII.

1950 – Alan Turing devises a test to determine if a machine exhibits intelligence indistinguishable from that of a human being. No machine has yet passed the Turing Test.

1954 – Researchers at Bell Labs create the world's first practical photovoltaic cell, converting sunlight into electricity.

1955 – The first atomic clock is developed using the regular vibrations of cesium atoms as an "atomic pendulum".

1963 – Does the flap of a butterfly's wings in Brazil set off a tornado in Texas? American meteorologist Edward Lorenz champions chaos theory—small changes in the initial conditions of some systems trigger widely different outcomes. These can be estimated but are fundamentally unpredictable.

1930   1940   1950   1960   1970

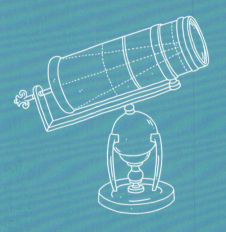

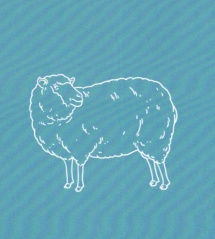

INFINITY
SKY & SPACE
1978 – *Space Invaders* video game is designed by Japanese developer Tomohiro Nishikado.
1983 – Subrahmanyan Chandrasekhar, an Indian astrophysicist, discovers that stars up to 1.4 times the size of the Sun will collapse to white dwarf stars as they age. Larger stars will become neutron stars or black holes.
1990 – The Hubble Space Telescope is maneuvered into orbit. Unimpeded by Earth's atmosphere, it is able to capture detailed images of deep space.
2014 – Spacecraft *Rosetta* lands a probe on a comet.
1977 – *Voyager 1* and *2* slingshot around the outer solar system taking spectacular pictures. In 2012, *Voyager 1* becomes the first artificial object to leave the solar system.
1998 – Assembly work begins on the International Space Station (ISS), a collaboration between the USA, Canada, Russia, Japan and European countries. When it launches in 2000, it will be the largest artificial object in orbit, visible by the naked eye from Earth.
2015 – The *New Horizons* space probe reaches Pluto.
1997 – NASA lands its first probe on Mars. It reveals dried-up riverbeds and ancient floodplains, suggesting there may have been life on Mars.
1983 – American aerospace company Lockheed develops the F-117A Nighthawk, the first airplane to use stealth technology to hide from radar.
1989 – The Montreal Protocol introduces a worldwide ban on the use of CFCs in an attempt to stop further damage being done to the Earth's ozone layer.
1994 – CFCs peak in the atmosphere but the ozone hole above the Antarctic is expected to heal by the year 2050, thanks to the phasing out of CFCs.
2003 – Concorde, the world's first supersonic airliner, is taken out of service after 27 years.
2017 – Completion of the International Space Station with the installation of the European Robotic Arm (ERA) and Multipurpose Laboratory Module.
TRANSPORT & COMMS
1981 – *Columbia* blasts off from Cape Canaveral in Florida, the first reusable spaceship. It is part of a fleet of five U.S. Space Shuttles, but two fatal accidents later blight the program.
1997 – *Thrust SSC*, a jet-propelled car driven by Andy Green, sets the land speed record at 763 mph. It is the first car officially to break the sound barrier.
2012 – Austrian skydiver Felix Baumgartner breaks the sound barrier skydiving from a helium balloon 29 miles above the Earth, reaching a speed of 843.6 mph.
PAN AM
BOEING 747
970 – A Boeing 747 umbo Jet" arrives in ondon after its maiden ght from x§New York.
– U.S. military scientists h the world's first packet- ning telecoms network, recursor to the Internet.
2001 – Segway PT, a two-wheeled, self-balancing, electric vehicle invented by Dean Kamen, is unveiled in New York. It uses gyroscopic sensors to balance upright.
2014 – Richard Noble designs a new supersonic car, *Bloodhound SSC*, that aims to be the first to top 1,000 mph.
1989 – British computer scientist Tim Berners-Lee invents the World Wide Web of interlinked documents accessed by a web browser.
2002 – General Motors produces Hy-wire, an electronically controlled concept car powered by hydrogen fuel cells.
facebook
2017 – Social media network Facebook, founded in 2004 by Mark Zuckerberg, boasts more than 1.86 billion active users worldwide with more than 300 million photos uploaded daily.
BUILDING & INVENTION
1973 – American inventor Dr. Martin Cooper, with a team from Motorola, develops the first cell phone.
1984 – A 1,970-foot-long railroad at Birmingham Airport is the first to use a commercial MAGLEV, magnetic levitation, system.
1990 – U.S. software giant Microsoft, founded by Bill Gates and Paul Allen, launches Windows 3.0—a graphical user interface that becomes the standard operating system on IBM-compatible PCs.
PRESS 'N PEEL?
1984 – Apple Computer, led by Steve Jobs, introduces its Macintosh, the first commercially successful computer to use a mouse and graphical-user interface.
IBM
Greetings from the Palm
DUBAI
2005 – British inventor James Dyson's bagless vacuum cleaners become the market leaders in the USA.
2016 - AlphaGo, a computer programme, becomes the first to beat a 9-dan professional player at the board game Go. Lee Sedol, from South Koren, loses four games to one.
1974 – American inventor Art Fry dreams up the Post-it note after experimenting with an adhesive previously thought too weak to have practical use. It is launched as Press 'n Peel three years later.
1981 – IBM introduces its 5150 personal computer.
1984 – A giant 1,700-foot flood barrier is built across the River Thames to protect London from high tides and surges.
1994 – Queen Elizabeth II and French President François Mitterrand open the Channel Tunnel to link England and France.
2001 – Construction begins on three artificial islands off the coast of Dubai. Palm Jumeirah, the first island, uses 123 million cubic yards of sand and 7.7 million tons of rock and becomes the world's largest artificial island.
2008 – A record two billion transistors are packed on a single microchip by Intel engineers. It is called the Tukwila quad-core processor.
ABCDEFGHIJKLMNOPQRS
EARTH & LAND
1978 – Lesley Brown gives birth to a daughter, Louise, the first person born as a result of *in vitro* fertilization (IVF). Pioneered by English physiologists Robert Edwards and Patrick Steptoe, this procedure inseminates an egg in a test tube and implants the embryo in the womb.
1994 – Genetically modified crops are introduced to improve resistance to disease and promote growth rate. Fears of consequences for humans and the environment lead to bans in some countries.
1997 – 55 nations are founder signatories to the Kyoto Protocol that sets binding obligations on industrialized nations to reduce emissions of greenhouse gases to avoid catastrophic climate change. Aviation and shipping are excluded and the USA refuses to sign.
GAIA
A NEW LOOK AT LIFE ON EARTH
1979 – James Lovelock publishes *Gaia*. He claims the Earth is like a self-regulating living organism that provides conditions for life to thrive.
1985 – The *Rainbow Warrior*, flagship of Greenpeace, the environmental protest organization, is sunk by French agents.
RAINBOW WARRIOR
MINERAL DEPOSITS
WATER SUPERHEATED BY MAGMA
1993 – The National Wind Technology center opens in Boulder, Colorado. The 305-acre site leads innovation in how best to use wind as a source of renewable energy.
INDUSTRY INC.
2005 – Chimpanzee DNA suggests the common ancestor of humans and their closest nonhuman relatives lived between five and seven million years ago.
GLOBAL SEA LEVEL PREDICTIONS
10,000?
400
300
200
100
YEARS
VENICE
SAN FRANCISCO
SHANGHAI
NEW YORK
260
3
SEA LEVEL RISE (FEET)
1977 – Scientists discover the presence of hydrothermal vents on the ocean floor —a possible habitat for the earliest life on Earth.
1996 – The Vacanti Mouse, created by American medic Dr. Charles Vacanti, has a cartilage structure grown on its back, made from cow cells, that looks like a human ear.
an Borlaug Nobel Peace eloping tant wheat widespread xico, India,
MEDICINE & BIOLOGY
SMALLPOX ERADICATED 26.10.1979
Raymond an Armenian- builds and Magnetic Imaging her. He he first can of eing five
1979 – Vaccination eradicates smallpox worldwide.
1983 – The HIV virus is identified as the causative agent of immune deficiency disease AIDS by French virologist Luc Montagnier.
HUMAN GENOME PROJECT
2003 – Researchers complete a multi-billion-dollar, 10-year-long Human Genome Project, designed to decode human DNA. Surprisingly, humans are found to have only about 21,000 genes, fewer than a rice plant.
2009 – Global warming in the 21st century is predicted to lead to sea level rises of between two and six feet. Technologies to control carbon dioxide levels may become essential to prevent runaway sea level rises and irreversable climate change.
AORTA
PULMONARY ARTERY
1982 – The first successful artificial heart, designed by American scientist Robert Jarvik, is fitted to Utah dentist Barney Clark.
ARTIFICIAL RIGHT VENTRICLE
ARTIFICIAL LEFT VENTRICLE
1996 – Ian Wilmut of the Roslin Institute in Scotland creates Dolly, the first cloned animal from a cell from a sheep's udder and another sheep's egg.
2012 – Synthetic meat is grown from stem cells in a Dutch laboratory, the first step toward more efficient production of meat than slaughtering animals.
2007 – American biologist James Thomson and Shinya Yamanaka of Kyoto University lead a team of researchers that successfully converts human skin cells into stem cells, potentially allowing the regeneration of all types of body tissues. The work avoids the ethical issue of having to harvest stem cells from human embryos.
DOROTHY HODGKIN
PHYSICS & CHEMISTRY
1977 – American biochemists Herbert Boyer and Stanley Cohen synthesize insulin using genetically modified bacteria. It is approved for use in treating diabetes in 1982.
INSULIN R
1984 – English geneticist Alec Jeffreys realizes that differences in individual's genetic codes can be used as key identification markers. His DNA fingerprinting technique is adopted worldwide by forensic police and genetic ancestry researchers.
1995 – American physicist Edward Witten unites attempts to reconcile gravity with quantum physics into a new universal theory of everything, called M-theory. The concept, which requires an 11-dimensional Universe, is supported by UK physicist Stephen Hawking but remains incomplete.
garian physicist Dennis ers holography—the d playback of images viewed from a range ngles as if they space.
REGULAR MATTER 4.6%
DARK MATTER 27%
DARK ENERGY 68%
DARK AGES
DEVELOPMENT OF GALAXIES
DARK ENERGY ACCELERATED EXPANSION
1ST STARS
13.7 BILLION YEARS
ra Rubin, an astronomer, galaxies spin according to aws of Motion fly apart. uggest they use of the gravity n particles dubbed r" which scientists akes up about 27% erse.
2004 – Physicists Andre Geim and Konstantin Novoselov isolate single atomic layers of graphite, called graphene, a highly electro-conductive material that is thin, light, stronger than steel, harder than diamonds, and 100 times more conductive than copper. Graphene may eventually be used to make everything from roll-up computer screens to cheap solar panels.
1990s – Physicists propose the existence of an unknown force called "dark energy" that may account for up to 68% of the total energy/mass in the Universe. The theory is needed to explain why the expansion of the Universe is accelerating.
1997 – Deep Blue, a super-computer built by IBM, defeats Russian world chess grandmaster Garry Kasparov. It is the first time a chess grandmaster has been beaten by a computer.
MATH & MEASUREMENT
1981 – Gerd Binnig and Heinrich Rohrer use quantum physics to develop the Scanning Tunneling Microscope (STM), which can observe and manipulate materials at the atomic level. They win the Nobel Prize in Physics five years later.
All Elliptic Curves are Modular
2013 – Scientists use a 17-mile doughnut-shaped underground particle accelerator called the Large Hadron Collider (LHC) to smash protons together at close to the speed of light. They find evidence of the mysterious particle called the Higgs boson (the "God particle") thought to give atomic particles mass.
1975 – International scientists finalize the Standard Model of subatomic particles. Evidence uncovered at CERN, the world's largest particle physics laboratory, shows the Universe is made up of quarks (matter particles) and bosons (force-carrying particles).
GRAVITY
STRONG
ELECTRO-MAGNETIC
WEAK
01
IBM
1995 – British mathematician Andrew Wiles proves Fermat's Last Theorem 358 years after it was first devised.
2010 – Polish-born mathematician Benoit Mandelbrot dies of cancer aged 85. He is remembered as the father of fractal geometry, a science of self-repeating patterns that becomes important in the production of computer-generated images, especially in the creation of computer games. They are also found throughout nature in lightning bolts, fault lines, and snowflakes.
972 – ewlett- ackard unches he HP-35, he first ocket cientific lectronic alculator.
1995 – A new system is launched for measuring time and location information in all weathers anywhere on Earth. The project, conceived by American scientist Roger Easton, uses a network of Global Positioning System satellites and is known as GPS.
1980 – Hungarian architect Erno Rubik licenses a twisting 3D puzzle for sale. The Rubik's Cube becomes one of the best-selling toys of all time.
2016 – An international team of physicists announces the detection of gravitational waves, ripples in spacetime first predicted by Albert Einstein.
51. 216814. 0. 239516
1980
1990
2000
2010
2020
ABSTRACT

Greek scientist takes giant leap!

BY OUR EUROPE EDITOR,
Syracuse, Sicily, ca. 250 BC

AN ECCENTRIC ENGINEER from Sicily was spotted yesterday charging naked down a public street toward the King's palace after leaping out of his bath shouting, *"Eureka! Eureka!"* ("I have found it! I have found it!")

Locals say the scientist, known as Archimedes, explained that his bizarre behavior had resulted from finding the solution to an intractable problem passed to him by royal officials.

King Hiero of Syracuse, Sicily, had given some gold to a goldsmith and asked him to make a wreath from it.

"But when it was finished, His Majesty suspected the goldsmith had pocketed some of the gold and replaced it with a cheaper metal," said Archimedes. "So he challenged me to find a way of proving whether the wreath was or was not made of pure gold."

Archimedes explained that he could only guarantee that the goldsmith had not cheated the King if he could determine beyond doubt that the original gold and the new wreath were the same weight and volume. They *were* the same weight, but how, wondered Archimedes, could one measure the volume of such an irregular shape as a metal wreath?

Archimedes says the answer came to him like a lightning bolt from the sky yesterday evening just as he was stepping into his bathtub.

"When I noticed how the water level rose as I sank deeper into the bath, I realized that if I measured the rise in the water when I placed the gold in the bath and compared it with the rise in water level when I placed the wreath in the bath, they should be the same."

However, initial findings indicated that the water levels were not the same, showing the wreath had been made with false materials. King Hiero has since had the goldsmith arrested.

Archimedes, a celebrated inventor of pulleys and water pumps, far from being reprimanded for streaking in public, is being hailed as a hero.

Chinese monks accidentally invent explosive powder

BY OUR CHINA STAFF, ca. AD 800

AN EXTRAORDINARY discovery is rumored to have been made by Taoist monks looking for a potion that would let people live forever.

The holy men are said to have been mixing honey, charcoal, realgar, sulfur, and saltpeter, only to have the recipe for immortality explode with such force that their hands and faces were burned and the house destroyed. The seriousness of their injuries is unknwon, but it is thought no lives were lost.

It seems profoundly ironic that it is here, in the tranquil heart of China, that these peace-loving monks performed their explosive experiment.

They were making the brew under instructions from the emperor, who is said to be desperate to secure for himself the prize of immortality.

Details of the monks' recipe have now reached officials in the military, who have plans to make weapons using the explosive powder.

Experts believe the new formula could transform the world. Some predict that the hugely destructive power of these compounds could even make warfare obsolete, as who would dare to confront an enemy equipped with such deadly fire?

However, others argue that if the secret of how to make the powder spreads, it could potentially lead to dangerous consequences.

Book of devices unveiled in Turkey

FROM OUR ASIA MINOR CORRESPONDENT, 1206

A REVOLUTIONARY new book that details as many as fifty extraordinary inventions, including pumps, clocks, robots, and washing machines, has been unveiled by Ismail al-Jazari, chief engineer at the Artuklu Palace in southeastern Turkey.

Intricate drawings illustrate an eclectic range of water-powered machines, including a waitress that can serve tea and drinks, a peacock fountain, complete with humanoid servants that can wash and dry people's hands, and what many consider to be one of his greatest masterpieces—an amazing elephant water-clock with animatronic musicians.

The elephant clock features a range of cultural influences, with the elephant representing India and Africa, the dragon China, the phoenix Egypt, and the turban Islam.

Experts believe that al-Jazari's *Book of Knowledge of Ingenious Mechanical Devices* may best be remembered for its depiction of the "crankshaft," a series of pins and connecting rods that turn rotation into linear motion.

Al-Jazari's crankshaft means that animals can be used to operate two-stroke cylinder water pumps, which is an innovation likely to be of immense value in boosting supplies of water on farms throughout the world.

Some speculate that al-Jazari's crankshaft could lead to the development of all kinds of extraordinary machines, in which mechanical controls even replace human labor. Indeed, al-Jazari's designs demonstrate just how advanced engineering and science skills have become in the thirteenth century.

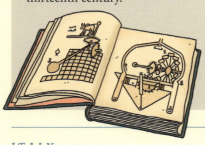

Numbers up for Italian trader

BY OUR ITALY DESK, Rome, 1202

TRADERS AND BANKERS will be able to make transactions and compute far more easily, thanks to the brilliant arithmetic method revealed in a groundbreaking new book.

Liber Abaci (which means "The Book of Calculation"), written by Italian merchant Leonardo of Pisa, also known as Fibonacci, explains a counting system first invented by Hindu mathematicians in India and then adopted by Arab merchants.

Instead of using Roman numerals, such as I, II, III, IV, V, VI, VII, VIII, IX, X, L, C, and M, the new system uses a single set of digits, 1, 2, 3, 4, 5, 6, 7, 8, and 9, to represent numbers.

Most revolutionary of all, the Arabic system incorporates a new number, "0" (pronounced zero), that has no value. According to Fibonacci, zero may be used as a placeholder to represent different orders of magnitude.

"With these nine figures, and with the sign 0, any number may be written," he notes.

Using the new number system, traditional Roman numerals, such as X, C, and M, can be represented using just two digits, 1 and 0. It means that MCMLXXXIV, for example, can be simplified into the number 1984.

Fibonacci's book also describes how these digits can represent fractions of numbers, thus greatly increasing the accuracy and flexibility of traditional arithmetic methods reliant on an old-fashioned abacus.

Commentators believe Fibonacci's book could transform all kinds of laborious tasks, from bookkeeping and the conversion of weights and measures to the calculation of interest and taxes.

The book also reveals how negative numbers can be used to keep track of loans and repayments, with the number 0 positioned in the middle of a number line.

One merchant from Florence said that after reading the book he was able to dispense entirely with his abacus. But another said he preferred more traditional methods of calculation.

Whichever technique today's traders prefer, Fibonacci's new number book looks as though it will have a profound impact on the world of Western trade and commerce.

Impressive printer spreads the word

BY OUR MEDIA CORRESPONDENT, Cologne, Germany, 1450

THE GENIUS INVENTOR Johannes Gutenberg is causing a reading revolution in Europe with his new machine—the printing press—which promises to make books far more widely available and affordable to the general public.

The secret of the new press is "movable type," in which metallic letters can be rearranged and reassembled, allowing Mr. Gutenberg to print all the pages of a book much faster than traditional techniques such as a scribe copying out a whole book by hand, which can take

many months. Another popular printing technique involves carving an entire page out of wood to use for pressing. However, these letters are not reusable, requiring each page to be crafted individually, so that a single spelling mistake from a careless woodcarver means having to remake the whole block.

Mr. Gutenberg says that his press was inspired by the wine presses of the grape-growing regions around his hometown of Mainz, Germany. It uses a massive wooden screw to press ink on the pages over the top of the printing plates, ensuring the pages print evenly. Mr. Gutenberg's invention is already creating a stir among printers throughout Europe.

Scientist claims Earth orbits Sun

FROM OUR ASTRONOMY EDITOR,
Rome, 1633

THE EXPECTED papal crackdown has finally fallen on an elderly Italian science scholar who is accused of undermining more than a thousand years of the church's teachings.

The Catholic Church has placed the best-selling book, entitled *Dialogue Concerning the Two Chief World Systems*, which was first published last year by the celebrated scientist Galileo Galilei, on its infamous Index of Forbidden Books. Yesterday Mr. Galileo was placed under house arrest on suspicion of heresy on the orders of Pope Urban VIII.

The dispute concerns a fierce debate about whether the Earth is stationary at the center of the Universe—as the church has always claimed—or whether, as Galileo suggests, the Earth is actually orbiting the Sun.

This extraordinary theory has been expounded by Mr. Galileo after experimenting with a new invention, the telescope, which reveals distant objects up to thirty times farther away than the naked eye can see.

The idea of the Earth orbiting the Sun—known as heliocentricity—follows on from the work of the Polish astronomer Nicolaus Copernicus, who first expounded the theory in his book *On the Revolutions of the Heavenly Spheres* in 1543. His book was also placed on the Catholic church's Index of Forbidden Books in 1616.

Mr. Galileo is thought to have become convinced that Mr. Copernicus was correct in his view that the Earth orbits the Sun after using his telescope to observe that Jupiter has four moons. Galileo's forbidden book suggests that, as the moons of Jupiter orbit Jupiter and not the Earth, the Earth can hardly be said to be at the center of the celestial system.

Catholic officials, however, are furious at the implication that church teachings are incorrect. As a result, the scientist has been ordered to stay at home under permanent armed guard and told to retract his views.

Dutchman swings pendulum for accuracy

A NEW CLOCK design was unveiled yesterday by the Dutch mathematician and physicist Christiaan Huygens, writes our horological correspondent from Amsterdam in 1656.

Mr. Huygens says his prototype clock, which uses a pendulum, can track the passage of time more accurately than any other available mechanism.

Mr. Huygens's pendulum forms the principal component in his invention. The pendulum consists of a weight suspended from a pivot, which swings back and forth with a "natural" frequency in the absence of pushes and pulls.

The mechanism has proved a very effective timekeeper, generating an inaccuracy of less than a minute a day—many other clocks fall behind by almost 15 minutes in the same period.

Mr. Huygens hopes his pendulum clock may one day be able to tell the time accurately even at sea aboard a rocking ship, although pendulums currently only operate when placed on a stable base.

The invention was inspired by Galileo Galilei's investigations into pendulums performed earlier in the century. Galileo discovered that the oscillation time of a pendulum remains the same regardless of the angle of its swing, a phenomenon known as isochronism.

The lark descending!

New book reveals a series of groundbreaking experiments, including one that proves living things cannot survive without air

BY OUR SCIENCE EDITOR,
London, 1660

A NEW BOOK has been released by alchemist and scientist Robert Boyle detailing his numerous and often astounding experiments with a mysterious "Pneumatical Engine." Improving upon earlier German designs for such a machine, Mr. Boyle has used his engine to investigate the strange properties of the air that surrounds us.

The machine uses a pump to "rarefy" or thin the air inside a glass chamber, creating a near-vacuum within. Mr. Boyle has used the machine to test the effect of this vacuum on a number of different objects, animals, and phenomena.

To date he has discovered that candles and coals do not burn in a vacuum. Another experiment involved placing a lark inside the chamber. It revealed that animals can easily become faint and will soon even die if the air is not quickly restored.

Some experts believe Mr. Boyle's new research, discussed in his book *Touching the Spring of the Air*, poses more exciting questions than answers. While his experiments with animals do give weight to the argument that a supply of air is needed for survival, some of his other studies have left even Mr. Boyle baffled.

One experiment involved dangling a constantly striking bell in the chamber.

The clapper continued to strike, but as the air was sucked out the sound faded away. This has led Mr. Boyle to theorize that air, though invisible, is in some way necessary to carry sound. Mr. Boyle also expected his coals and candles to burn brighter in the vacuum, as no air was present to obstruct combustion.

However, he found the opposite to be true and is as yet unable to account fully for the phenomenon. Mr. Boyle is known to be a cautious scientist, unwilling to put forward theories about which he cannot be sure. His investigations are already spurring on a new generation of budding scientists.

Light dawns as apple falls for super-scientist

"I realized that an apple falls to the ground as a result of an invisible force," says scientist

BY OUR INNOVATION EDITOR ,
Cambridge, England, July 6, *1687*

WHAT IS THE MEANING of life, the Universe, and everything? The question has puzzled philosophers, monks, and scientists for centuries, but now Isaac Newton, a scientist from Cambridge, England, has proposed a new theory after simply witnessing an apple falling to the ground from a tree.

Since the dawn of time people have wondered about the mysteries of the Universe—for example, what causes the movements of the planets in the night sky? Are they moving randomly or is there some other logic or force driving their motion?

Mr. Newton's answer is revealed in a new book published yesterday called *Principia Mathematica*. It outlines how the movement of everything, from a leaf fluttering to the ground to planets whirling in space, can be explained by three laws of motion and a mysterious invisible force called gravity.

Mr. Newton says the revelation came to him one summer's day in 1666 in Woolsthorpe, Lincolnshire, where he had fled from Cambridge after an outbreak of the Great Plague. "I realized that an apple falls to the ground as a result of an invisible force—and that this same force is responsible for keeping the planets in orbit around the Sun. Just as gravity pulls the apple to the ground, so it keeps the Moon and planets in their orbits instead of flying off into space."

According to Mr. Newton, this invisible gravity is an all-pervasive force that behaves the same way everywhere in the Universe. He claims that its strength can be worked out from the masses of different objects and the square of the distance separating them.

Mr. Newton's three laws of motion can be summarized as follows: 1) an object will continue to stay still or move at a constant speed and in a constant direction unless another force acts on it; 2) the rate of change in the velocity of an object is directly related to the strength of the force that is causing the change; and 3) any two objects acting on each other will exert equal and opposite forces. As a result of Mr. Newton's theories, the motion of objects anywhere in the Universe can be predicted with great accuracy.

Aside from his grand unifying theory, Mr. Newton is also an alchemist and an inventor of telescopes. He has even proved how white light is made up of a spectrum of all the different colors in a rainbow by shining a beam of sunlight through a prism.

Furthermore, Mr. Newton claims to have invented his own branch of mathematics to predict how fast objects will accelerate, slow down, or change direction. However, a German mathematician named Gottfried Leibniz has challenged the claim, saying he was first to develop the system, which is known as calculus.

Fellow scientists and disciples of the pair have begun taking sides, with some believing Mr. Newton's assertion that he developed the system in his youth but never published it, while others think Mr. Newton got his ideas from an earlier work by Leibniz.

Regardless of the truth, calculus is already proving vital for working with Mr. Newton's investigations into the forces of motion.

Many commentators believe that the combination of Mr. Newton's astonishing theory of gravity and his innovation in mathematics may herald the start of a new era of scientific enlightenment.

Harrison clocks success, but still all at sea

BY OUR HOROLOGICAL
CORRESPONDENT, London, *1736*

A SELF-EDUCATED clockmaker from Wakefield yesterday took the first step toward solving the Longitude Problem, the problem of how to accurately calculate the east–west or "longitudinal" position of a vessel at sea.

John Harrison believes his new device, the marine chronometer, may offer a solution after it was recently used to accurately measure a ship's location while at sea.

Mr. Harrison's solution lies in creating a clock that does not use a traditional pendulum—allowing it to be a reliable timekeeper even on rough seas. The special clock is used to calculate longitudinal position by comparing the time calibrated at the point of departure with the local time as shown by the position of the Sun and stars at any point while at sea.

While many others agree with his solution, skepticism exists regarding the creation of a reliable timekeeper that will work at sea. Even the late, great Isaac Newton said he doubted such a clock was buildable, as it must be able to resist the effects of changing temperatures and humidity, strong winds and rocking ships—no small feat.

Instead of a pendulum, Mr. Harrison's new clock uses a specially designed system of brass balances. Using two equally weighted balances allows one to counteract the movement of the other even when the ship rolls.

On a recent trip, returning to England from Lisbon, Portugal, Mr. Harrison used his ingenious device to correct navigational errors and accurately predict the point of the ship's arrival.

However, the true test of Mr. Harrison's machine will be on an Atlantic crossing. Mr. Harrison is now petitioning the government for a grant to start work on an improved clock capable of making the ocean crossing. If successful he could claim the $30,000 prize offered to whoever can solve the Longitude Problem.

Engineer builds up steam for a revolution

A PATENT for a revolutionary new type of steam engine has been lodged by James Watt, a steam engineer from Greenock in Scotland, writes our technology correspondent in 1781.

The new engine uses an external condenser, which vastly improves the efficiency of existing designs by steam pioneer Thomas Newcomen. It also features an innovative fly-wheel to convert linear into rotary motion, promising to transform how steam engines can be used for everything from making cotton to transporting people, and paving the way for a mechanical renaissance.

Unlike previous steam engines, which produce a pumping action and are frequently used to drain mines, Mr. Watt's flywheel system produces rotational power. His innovative gears are attached to the engine by a bar that travels around and turns the fixed flywheel creating rotary motion.

Experts believe that Mr. Watt's invention will allow the use of steam power in factories, further stoking the industrial revolution that is underway. Mr. Watt has come up with a new measure—called "horsepower"—for the power of his engines, comparing their brute mechanical strength to the power of animals.

Paris liftoff means sky is no longer out of reach

An age of aviation beckons as humans take safely to the skies

BY OUR AVIATION EDITOR,
Paris, September 22, 1783

A TEACHER and an army officer from France yesterday became the first people to fly in an air balloon not attached to the ground by a tether. The two men, Jean-François Pilâtre de Rozier and Marquis François Laurent d'Arlandes, landed safely after an extraordinary 25-minute balloon flight that carried them from the western outskirts of Paris for a distance of about five miles at 3,000 feet above the Earth.

The historic flight follows a test run two months ago in which a balloon took off from the Palace of Versailles —with a sheep, duck, and rooster on board to show that living creatures would not be harmed by high altitudes.

Joseph-Michel and Jacques-Étienne Montgolfier, paper manufacturers from the Ardèche, are the geniuses behind the extraordinary achievement of taking humans into the air and landing them back safely.

The idea of creating a balloon powered by hot air that could rise up above the Earth came to Joseph Montgolfier after he observed how the pockets of his trousers would billow upwards when drying over a fire.

"I came to believe that within the smoke of a fire is a special kind of gas that makes things rise up," he said. "So I began thinking about how to design a machine that could be used to lift people into the air."

After much experimentation and many false starts, the brothers succeeded in making a balloon out of silk lined with a varnish of alum to make it fire resistant. This was used for the test flight of the animals from Versailles earlier this year.

A new balloon around 75 feet tall, called *Le Globe Aérostatique*, was then constructed for yesterday's flight. The balloon was ornately decorated in blue and gold, with signs of the zodiac around the edges and portraits of King Louis XVI in the center.

The American ambassador to France, Dr. Benjamin Franklin, attended the historic flight.

"We observed it lift off in the most majestic manner," he reported. "When it reached around 250 feet in altitude, the intrepid voyagers lowered their hats to salute the spectators. We could not help feeling a certain mixture of awe and admiration."

Lavoisier remembered as father of chemistry

ANTOINE LAVOISIER, one of the greatest scientists of all time, yesterday became the latest victim of revolutionary France's brutal guillotine, *writes our Paris editor on May 9, 1794.*

Mr. Lavoisier was best known for his investigations into the element of air called oxygen, a substance that he proved is fundamental to combustion and respiration. He used his discoveries to disprove the long-standing Phlogiston Theory that claimed that certain materials contain a strange substance

Huge loss for scientific community as revolutionary forces sweep through France

called Phlogiston that is allegedly released when things catch fire.

Mr. Lavoisier is also famous for recognizing and naming another gas, "hydrogen," which means "water-former," after he proved that burning it alongside oxygen creates water. This experiment demonstrated the bizarre fact that water, a liquid at room temperature, is composed of two elements that are gases at room temperature—hydrogen and oxygen.

Mr. Lavoisier will also be remembered for putting together one of the first tables of elements and forming his own theory of combustion, as outlined in his book *Elementary Treatise on Chemistry.* The ideas contained within the work

have since forced scientists across the world to reevaluate their views on the chemical elements, despite opposition from supporters of the now-debunked Phlogiston Theory.

Although his reputation as a scientist was exemplary, Mr. Lavoisier's work for the prerevolution government of France made him many enemies. Branded a traitor by the fanatical politician Maximilien Robespierre earlier this year, Mr. Lavoisier has now become another tragic victim of the French Revolution.

Curious doctor pioneers deadly pox protection

Experiments on child, disease never develops

BY OUR MEDICAL CORRESPONDENT,
Berkeley, England, 1796

A DOCTOR FROM ENGLAND has conducted medical trials on an eight-year-old boy in an attempt to develop a way of protecting people against smallpox, the world's most deadly disease.

Dr. Edward Jenner believes his new treatment may put a stop to the dreadful "pox," a disease that has killed millions of people with a frighteningly high rate of death among those infected.

Dr. Jenner, who practices in England, says that he noticed that milkmaids were among the few groups of people who seemed rarely to catch the hideous disease. Realizing that this might be linked to an immunity developed by contracting the milder disease of cowpox, he decided to test his theory.

However, his choice of a healthy eight-year-old boy, James Phipps, as his test subject has raised some eyebrows. Luckily for the youngster, and the reputation of Dr. Jenner, the trial was a success. After infecting the boy with cowpox, Dr. Jenner

found, to the relief of James and his parents, that he was miraculously immune to the deadly smallpox. Dr. Jenner tried to infect James several times with smallpox, but, fortunately for the boy and his family, the disease never developed.

Dr. Jenner has now repeated the experiment on another twenty-three test subjects, all of whom have remained perfectly healthy. Armed with proof that his immunization technique works, Dr. Jenner has released his findings in a study.

He argues that his method, known as vaccination (named for the Latin *vacca*—"cow," referring to the source of the milder "cowpox"), replaces the old and less reliable immunization method known as variolation or inoculation.

This old method, which involves taking the greasy pus and scabs from unfortunate sufferers of smallpox and rubbing it into small cuts in the skin, was first brought to Europe from Turkey in 1714. However, it is potentially deadly as the subject can sometimes develop fully fledged smallpox. Dr. Jenner says his method involves no such risks.

Dr. Jenner's pioneering vaccination technique is already creating a buzz since experts think

it may be possible to use it to prevent other deadly diseases. Infecting an individual with a related but less dangerous disease could provide an effective way of educating people's immune systems, they believe.

Medical practioners are expressing great interest in the concept of vaccination. With powerful supporters and his successful experiments, Dr. Jenner's dream of a world free of many of the most virulent diseases may soon become a real possibility.

New mechanical computer makes math simple

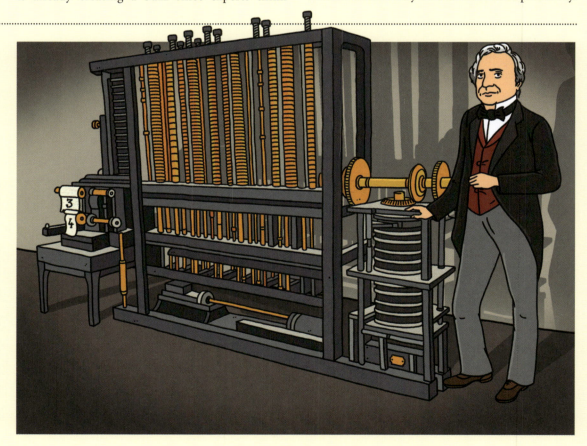

A MACHINE that could one day wipe out the need for humans to do complex sums is to be built by engineering genius Charles Babbage, *writes our technology editor from London in 1822.*

Yesterday, the British government advanced more than $1,500 for work to start on the project in which a machine, known as the Difference Engine, will calculate logarithmic tables without the need for human intervention.

Logarithmic tables help save work and time when performing laborious multiplication and division calculations. They are, for instance, used by military engineers to help work out the trajectory of ballistics so that munitions can be fired with greater accuracy.

Mr. Babbage believes computers may one day fully automate mathematical calculation.

Inventor puts painters out of the picture

A NEW TECHNIQUE that will enable scientists to produce accurate pictures without drawing, painting, or etching has been developed in France, writes our arts editor from Paris in 1826.

French inventor Nicéphore Niépce has used his method of "heliography" to create images of the landscape surrounding his country estate in eastern France. Mr. Niépce first used his process four years ago to make an image of Pope Pius VII, but this was destroyed after he attempted to make prints from it.

Heliography, or "sun-drawing," uses light and a device known as a "camera obscura," a box with a tiny hole on one side. A tar-like compound called Bitumen of Judea is applied to a metal plate placed inside the camera obscura.

Light travels into the box via the hole and projects an image onto the plate inside. Where the tar is exposed to light it hardens. But on unexposed surfaces the tar remains soft, and it can be rinsed off. This leaves an image on the plate's surface, and reveals bright, sunlit objects against shadows.

Sky's not the limit for stargazer's success

BY OUR ASTRONOMY EDITOR,
London, England, 1828

THE ROYAL ASTRONOMICAL SOCIETY has announced the award of its prestigious Gold Medal to the well-known astronomer Caroline Herschel, celebrated for discovering comets and creating a catalog of stars and their positions. This is the first time the award has been made to a woman. Miss Herschel is also the first woman to hold an official position with the British government, and the first known female to be paid for her work as a scientist and astronomer.

The prize recognizes Miss Herschel's career as a scientist in her own right after years of working alongside her brother William. It is widely known that the star catalog published in 1802 by the Royal Society under his name was in fact almost completely the work of his sister. It added 500 new star clusters a n d nebulae to the 2,000 previously known to exist.

Miss Herschel's unique independent contribution to astronomy was acknowledged some years ago when she spent a week as the personal guest of the royal family in Greenwich, London—both King George and Queen Charlotte were very interested in the sciences.

Miss Herschel has had to fight prejudice against professional women, still very much a feature of Georgian England as elsewhere in the world. She also faced big challenges earlier in her life after contracting the disease typhus when she was ten. This led to poor vision in her left eye and limited her growth to just over four feet tall.

Fortunately, vision in Miss Herschel's right eye is exceptionally good. Although she first started working with William to keep records of his work, it became clear Miss Herschel had a genius for interpreting and writing about astronomical observations and also was extremely good at spotting new distant objects in the sky. To do this required hours perched on a ladder to reach the eyepiece of the 40-foot and 20-foot reflecting telescopes at Observatory House near Windsor, the home of William, his wife Mary, and son John.

Caroline and William Herschel were born in the German town of Hanover, King George's family home. They traveled to England to take advantage of their hometown's royal connections.

Electric discovery sparks motor revolution

MICHAEL FARADAY this week stunned the scientific world with a series of experimental demonstrations at the Royal Institution in London, *writes our science correspondent on August 30, 1831.*

He showed that electricity can be generated in a coil of wire by moving a magnet in and out of it. Previously, electric currents have only been created using a voltaic pile, a type of chemical battery named after its Italian inventor, Alessandro Volta, who came up with the concept in 1800.

But the ability to stimulate an electric force using nothing more than a magnet opens up all kinds of new possibilities for how electricity may be generated in the future.

Mr. Faraday's experiment, known as electromagnetic induction, follows another extraordinary discovery he unveiled at the Royal Institution ten years ago. This showed how electricity could be made to rotate a wire, the first ever public demonstration of the principle of an electric motor.

Some experts believe these two phenomena have the potential to create a world where electric forces replace many of today's mechanical and steam-driven devices.

Mr. Faraday claims that the electromagnetic effects demonstrated in his experiments are caused by "lines of force" that can be shown graphically by the patterns of iron filings around a magnet.

However, many experts are still struggling to accept the idea that a semi-mystical invisible force without mass can be responsible for such profound effects, especially as no mathematical principles have yet been discovered to account for the phenomenon.

Humans and apes have common descent

BY OUR NATURE EDITOR,
Kent, England, 1859

A NEW BOOK claiming to reveal the inner workings of life on Earth has been published by Charles Darwin, a naturalist living in Kent, England.

The book makes the astonishing claim that all forms of life share a common ancestor—including humans, who share prehistoric ancestors with modern apes!

Mr. Darwin's book, *On the Origin of Species by Means of Natural Selection*, proposes that life evolves over many generations through a process in which those living things best adapted to environmental conditions thrive, while those less well adapted suffer, eventually becoming extinct. "From so simple a beginning," he writes, "endless forms most beautiful and most wonderful have been, and are being, evolved."

The book is causing uproar among religious leaders, who refuse to accept that humans and apes share a common ancestor. They also argue that since—according to the Bible—the world is only 5,000 years old, there is not enough time for Mr. Darwin's "evolution" to have occurred.

School of nursing opens thanks to a Nightingale

War hero's statistics prove that good hygiene is key to good health

BY OUR MEDICAL EDITOR,
London, England, 1860

NURSING PIONEER Florence Nightingale saw her lifetime ambition fulfilled yesterday with the opening of the world's first training school for professional nurses, based at St. Thomas' Hospital, London.

Miss Nightingale, also known as the Lady of the Lamp, is famous for running a war hospital that used teams of nurses patrolling wards of injured soldiers day and night. However, Miss Nightingale is now campaigning to improve human welfare and has developed a reputation as a formidable statistician.

The daughter of a wealthy upper-class English family, Miss Nightingale says she had an instinctive calling to use her wealth, education, and intellect to help others. In 1854 she volunteered to work in a war zone hospital during the Crimean War. There she led a team of 53 volunteer nurses and nuns in appalling conditions, but realized that improved hygiene, food, and living conditions were key to saving soldiers' lives.

Miss Nightingale's meticulous records of causes of death have now been carefully analyzed using statistical charts, known as Coxcombs. They reveal in graphic detail the awful truth that ten times as many troops died from malnutrition, poor sanitation and inactivity than enemy action.

The Crimean War (1853 to 1856) saw British, French, and Ottoman Turkish allies fighting Russia for control of the Crimean Peninsula and surrounding lands on the shores of the Black Sea. For the first time, newspapers reported on the horrendous conditions soldiers were living in and they detailed Nightingale's groundbreaking research into the unnecessary loss of life.

Government officials responded to Miss Nightingale's findings by sending a prefabricated hospital, designed by leading engineer Isambard Kingdom Brunel, to the frontline to help improve conditions for soldiers. Among new volunteers was Mary Seacole. Fiercely proud of both her Jamaican and Scottish ancestry, Mrs. Seacole nursed soldiers on the front line and was a strong supporter of Miss Nightingale's efforts to save lives.

Miss Nightingale's new training school means that nurses will now be recruited from all levels of society where previously the profession was reserved for women in the lowest and poorest of circumstances. They will be properly trained in the benefits of good hygiene, one of the greatest medical discoveries of all time.

Elementary idea solves order of chemicals

BY OUR RUSSIA STAFF,
St. Petersburg, March 7, 1869

A SIBERIAN CHEMIST last night unveiled an ingenious new way to order the chemical elements, by placing them in a table that makes sense of their properties.

Dmitri Mendeleev was amazed to notice a series of recurring patterns within the sixty-three known elements while writing a new textbook titled Principles of Chemistry. *He is said to have made his discovery while playing Solitaire with a pack of cards.*

He realized that by ordering all the elements by increasing atomic weight, a pattern emerged in which every seventh element lined up into a group with other elements that shared similar characteristics. Gaps in the table suggest the existence of various elements that have yet to be discovered.

By looking at the places where the gaps occur, Mr. Mendeleev believes it may be possible to predict the properties and reactivity of the missing elements. Mr. Mendeleev says his greatest inspiration has been gained from hard work. "Pleasures flit by, they are only for yourself," he explains. "Work leaves a mark of long-lasting joy." Scientists predict that the Periodic System, as Mr. Mendeleev has called it, will underpin a new understanding of the elements.

Bell rings for long-distance telephones

BY OUR MEDIA EDITOR,
Boston, March 11, 1876

LONG-DISTANCE VOICE communications between people all over the world may soon become a reality thanks to the efforts of the inventor Alexander Graham Bell.

A patent granted by the United States Patent Office describes a device that allows a person to speak into a machine at one end of a telegraph line and another person to hear their words at the other end of the line.

Yesterday, in Boston, Mr. Bell was able to make his device work for the first time, relaying a message to his assistant in an adjoining room. "I shouted into M [the mouthpiece] the following sentence: 'Mr. Watson, come here, I want to see you!' To my delight he came and declared that he had heard and understood what I said."

Meanwhile, a dispute has broken out between Mr. Bell and Elisha Gray, an engineer from Barnesville, Ohio, who claims that Mr. Bell stole a design for a water-based variable resistor mechanism used to turn sound waves into electromagnetic signals.

Lawyers representing both parties are now arguing over the validity of Mr. Bell's claim to have invented the telephone.

Prolific inventor makes light work

"I have not failed, I have found ten thousand ways that do not work," said electric pioneer

BY OUR TECHNOLOGY EDITOR,
New York, September 5, 1882

THE RELENTLESS determination of inventor Thomas Edison paid off yesterday when he announced what may be his biggest achievement yet—a privately owned electricity transmission network connecting fifty-nine households in Pearl Street, New York City.

"Finally, I won't have to worry any more about gas leaks killing us all in our beds," said one happy customer last night.

Thanks to earlier work carried out by Mr. Edison, electric lightbulbs connected to the new network can be used by customers to replace candles and gas lamps. Mr. Edison publicly demonstrated this revolutionary technology three years ago at his world-leading research center at Menlo Park, New Jersey.

Mr. Edison has a huge reputation as one of our most persistent inventors. Once, when a journalist challenged him as to why he had failed to invent a lightbulb that didn't explode every time it was attached to an electrical circuit, Mr. Edison is said to have exclaimed, "I have not failed, I have found ten thousand ways that do not work!"

It is to such persistence that many attribute Mr. Edison's numerous achievements to date. These include the quadruplex telegraph (allowing more than one signal to be sent over a telegraph wire at a time), the carbon microphone (for use in telephones), a durable, reusable incandescent electric lightbulb (using a filament made of carbonized bamboo), the phonograph (for recording and playing back sounds), and ticker tape (for transmitting the prices of stocks and shares over telegraph lines).

Four years ago Mr. Edison created the Edison Electric Light Company, which now owns his many patents. Funding from powerful U.S. businessmen such as J. P. Morgan and the Vanderbilts has allowed Mr. Edison and his team to follow their dreams of developing electrical transmission.

According to the inventor, electricity will soon be so cheap even smelly tallow candles will seem expensive. With such ambition, Mr. Edison and his engineers look set to light up the world.

Aviators take Wright turn

BY OUR AVIATION EDITOR,
Kitty Hawk, North Carolina,
December 18, 1903

A PAIR OF BICYCLE-shop owners from Dayton, Ohio, yesterday demonstrated the first-ever machine-powered, heavier-than-air human flight. They made two flights, lasting 12 seconds and 59 seconds, in an experimental aircraft named the Flyer, which took off and landed safely at Kitty Hawk, North Carolina.

Five onlookers witnessed the remarkable propeller-powered plane take to the air. Its innovative lightweight engine was designed and built by the Wrights' bicycle workshop mechanic, Charlie Taylor.

Wilbur and Orville Wright have spent the last four years in their bicycle workshop trying to discover how to power and control an aircraft that can carry a human being. They even drew inspiration from the celebrated Renaissance artist Leonardo da Vinci,

who is famous for having drawn detailed sketches of futuristic flying machines.

To stabilize their aircraft, the Wright brothers have devised a "wing-warping" control mechanism that mimics how birds change direction in flight by angling the ends of their wings. A system of cables pulls the ends of the aircraft's wings in opposite directions

so the plane can bank more easily when changing direction, increasing its stability.

For the last three years, the Wright brothers have been conducting secret test flights with a series of homemade gliders at Kitty Hawk. U.S. officials are now said to be interested in the technology's military potential.

World mourns hero of science

BY OUR CHEMISTRY CORRESPONDENT,
Paris, July 5, 1934

MARIE CURIE, considered to be one of the world's greatest scientists, died yesterday at a sanatorium, in southeastern France. She was 66.

Professor Curie was the first woman professor at the Sorbonne University, Paris, the first woman to receive the Nobel Prize, and the only person to win two Nobel Prizes in different fields of science, physics and chemistry.

She will be remembered most of all for her famous discovery of the elements of radium and polonium along with work on radioactivity and its use to treat tumors. She died of aplastic anemia, which some

believe was caused by years of handling radioactive material before realizing its dangers.

Born Maria Salomea Skłodowska in 1867 in Warsaw, Poland, she became a student of the secret Flying University, which taught students, including women, science, a subject banned by the authorities.

At age 24 Maria traveled to France and met and married fellow scientist Pierre Curie in 1885. They worked as a team until 1906 when Pierre was tragically struck and killed by a horse-drawn vehicle.

Throughout her career Professor Curie turned down prizes and didn't take out patents on her discoveries. Famous physicist Albert Einstein said, "Marie Curie is, of all celebrated beings, the only one fame has not corrupted."

Einstein warns of race to develop a nuclear bomb

BY OUR SCIENCE EDITOR,
New York, October 12, 1939

THE WORLD-FAMOUS physicist Albert Einstein has sent an urgent letter to the President of the United States, Franklin D. Roosevelt, warning him against the terrible dangers posed by new research into atomic forces.

Dr. Einstein and his colleague Dr. Leo Szilard told the President of the potential for enemy nations to build a nuclear bomb using radioactive uranium that may be capable of causing destruction on an unprecedented scale.

The two scientists have advised the President that the United States should gather together the best possible team of scientists and engineers to conduct its own research into this field. Their call is made all the more pressing because it is thought that Nazi Germany may be developing its own nuclear weapon as the specter of war looms over Europe.

The scientists' concern stems from experiments performed last year in Berlin that demonstrated the process of nuclear fission or "splitting the atom" for the first time, a process they say could be used peacefully, for energy production, or aggressively— to construct a devastating weapon of mass destruction.

The process relies upon a natural law identified by Dr. Einstein himself in 1905. The law states that mass and energy are convertible, and that an

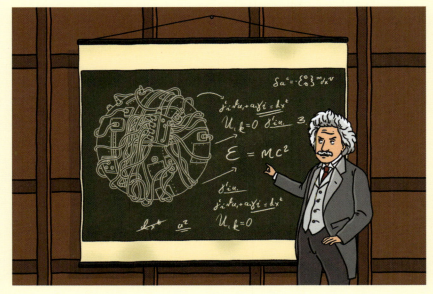

object's mass can be expressed as an amount of energy, and vice versa.

Dr. Einstein expressed this through the simple formula $E=mc^2$—whereby E, the energy, is equal to the mass multiplied by c, the speed of light, squared. This means that, since light travels at such a monumental speed, even objects with a small mass contain colossal quantities of energy. According to Dr. Einstein, the amount of energy locked inside the atoms of just one grain of sand is enough to boil a pot of water 10 billion times!

Nuclear fission "splits" a heavy atom in two by bombarding it with neutrons, small particles that carry no electrical charge. This releases more neutrons, which continue the process of splitting atoms, releasing vast quantities of energy.

Dr. Einstein, without question one of the defining physicists of this century, has focused his research on areas where Isaac Newton's laws have been found not to function as expected. By delving into these areas, he has revolutionized scientific thought, particularly through his special and general theories of relativity, which relate to the fundamental forces of electromagnetism and gravity.

Dr. Einstein's work on the photoelectric effect, whereby electrons are ejected from a metal under light, overturned the classical explanation for light energy and earned him the 1921 Nobel Prize in Physics.

President Roosevelt is believed to be taking Dr. Einstein's warnings very seriously indeed.

World War survivor's invention adds up

IMAGINE a machine that can do any calculation in the world and that you can also hold in the palm of your hand! That's the genius result of a decade-long quest by a war survivor who has built an extraordinary pocket mechanical calculator, writes our technology editor in 1948.

The "Curta" is the brainchild of Viennese machine-whiz Curt Herzstark. Its ingenious barrel design contains all the cogs and gears required for addition, subtraction, multiplication, and division.

Mr. Herzstark had patented a similar design in 1938, but his work was interrupted by the outbreak of World War II, during which period he was arrested and sent to a concentration camp.

It was while in the camp that Mr. Herzstark wrote down the intricate designs required to make his amazing machine. After being released in 1945, he traveled to a small country called Lichtenstein, on the border with Austria, where his stunning invention was eventually manufactured.

Double twist as DNA discovery unlocks secrets of genetic science

BY OUR MEDICAL EDITOR,
Cambridge, England, April 26, 1953

SCIENTISTS CLAIM to have unraveled one of the biggest mysteries of life following many years of research into the chemical code inside living cells called "DNA" (deoxyribonucleic acid).

A whole team of experts, including Dr. Rosalind Franklin and Dr. Maurice Wilkins, have been making important discoveries about the composition of DNA using diffraction by X-ray crystallography. One such image produced by Dr. Franklin has been key to new developments by Dr. James Watson and Mr. Francis Crick.

Yesterday, Dr. Watson and Mr. Crick published their discoveries about the structure of the DNA molecule, which is widely thought to be the key to understanding how life has evolved. A unique pattern or sequence of DNA is present in the cells of every living creature, inherited from its parents. In humans, DNA carries genetic instructions for everything from the color of our eyes to the chances of developing certain diseases.

Developing a model for the structure of DNA is thought to be fundamental to understanding how the process

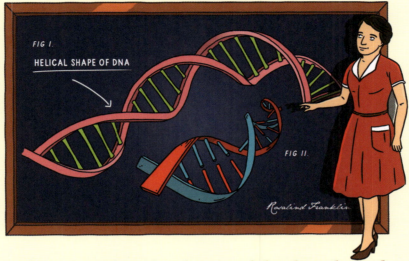

FIG I.
HELICAL SHAPE OF DNA

FIG II.

Rosalind Franklin

"The DNA molecule is widely thought to be the key to understanding how life has evolved"

of inheriting or not inheriting these characteristics takes place. Once the structure is known, experts believe it is only a matter of time before humans can manipulate DNA, perhaps helping to cure hereditary diseases.

Dr. Watson and Mr. Crick used cardboard cutouts of the DNA molecule's components to produce hypothetical arrangements for the structure. They found that the components of DNA exist in two long, intertwined segments, bonded across

the center, forming a twisting "double helix." The order of the components in each segment determines how the genes in a living organism are expressed.

Knowing the structure of DNA will allow medical science to better understand where personal traits come from and potentially, in the case of hereditary diseases, how to counter them. Perhaps most exciting, however, is the light it may shed on the origins of life and its diversification over billions of years.

Personal desktop computer hits home

BY OUR TECHNOLOGY EDITOR,
Boca Raton, Florida, August 13, 1981

THE WORLD'S biggest and most successful manufacturer of computers yesterday announced the release of its first-ever personal desktop.

International Business Machines (IBM) hopes that its new 5150 Personal Computer will revolutionize how people think about computers and will expand the role they play in everyday life.

In 1943 Thomas Watson, then chairman of IBM, said that he felt "there is a world market for maybe five computers." Now his computer company has become hugely successful, selling thousands of machines worldwide. However, until now IBM has focused on huge "mainframe" computers, capable of performing complex calculations and predictions for big businesses.

Mainframes are expensive and bulky, and require a team of dedicated staff and often a special air-controlled room of their own. But the new Personal Computer (nicknamed a "PC") is set to bring the computer into the home, increasing its ease of use and making it a regular household object.

IBM's new machine follows the pioneering work of Henry "Ed" Roberts, who developed some of the world's first electronic calculators and launched the Altair 8800 microcomputer in 1974.

Priced at around $1,500, IBM's new PC is affordable enough for individuals other than dedicated hobbyists to consider buying one, and small enough not to need a basement conversion just to fit it in the house.

One of the biggest benefits of a PC over a conventional typewriter is that errors are not permanent and multiple copies can be rapidly printed out using a small desktop printer.

Among the PC's most innovative features, however, is its operating system (the software communicating between the user and the computer hardware). This code, called MS-DOS, has been designed by the programmer Bill Gates and his team at Microsoft. It has been engineered for ease of use, so that nontechnical people can easily pick up how to use a PC, and so that developers can easily write new software applications.

Computer engineer spins a global world wide web

BY OUR COMPUTER EDITOR,
Geneva, Switzerland, August 7, 1991

A FAST WAY for people to publish information on the computer network known as the Internet has been pioneered by British physicist and telecommunications engineer Tim Berners-Lee.

The system, dubbed the World Wide Web, allows words and pictures hosted on different computers to be linked together on a web page. A collection of web pages, known as a website, was yesterday demonstrated at CERN, the European particle accelerator beneath the French–Swiss border, where Mr. Berners-Lee is a fellow.

In March 1989, Mr. Berners-Lee developed a proposal for a new computer system at CERN, which was originally intended to improve communication and information sharing between researchers.

The World Wide Web uses a hypertext system that allows web pages to be connected to each other by easily navigable "links." Its potential applications stretch much further than simply organizing information. For example, ordering your shopping or buying your favorite music through a home computer may one day be possible.

The new CERN website—the world's first—will act as a launchpad for the Web's expansion, providing instructions on how individuals can set up their own servers and web pages. Anyone with Internet access can see it at: info.cern.ch.

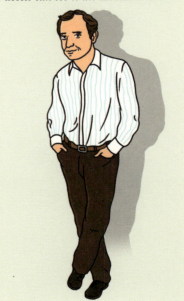

Hello, Dolly! Scientific breakthrough spells hope for world's endangered species

BY OUR TECHNOLOGY EDITOR,
Edinburgh, Scotland, February 23, 1997

A TEAM of scientists at the University of Edinburgh, Scotland, yesterday announced the birth of the world's most remarkable sheep. Dolly is the first healthy mammal to have been born as a result of cloning from an adult cell.

The cloning process produces offspring from the DNA of a single animal parent. Unlike sexual reproduction, which combines the DNA of two parents, scientists created Dolly by carefully inserting the DNA of a single adult sheep into an unfertilized egg from another sheep.

This egg was then implanted into the womb of a third sheep. Although Dolly technically has three mothers, all her genes come from only one.

Scientists chose a white-faced Finn-Dorset sheep to be the DNA provider and two Scottish black-faced sheep for the egg and the surrogate mother. When Dolly was born with a white face, they knew immediately the experiment had been a success.

The technique, known as nuclear transfer, is delicate. Scientists first

Pioneering method shows that humans can now manipulate life's most delicate processes

remove the tiny nucleus from an adult cell—in this case from the udder—using a micropipette, a syringe only the width of a hair. This nucleus, which contains the DNA, is then placed into the egg of another sheep, which has had its nucleus removed. Small electric pulses are used to trigger the development process. Once the embryo starts to grow, it is implanted in a womb. Months later the lamb is born. This process is so delicate that

Dolly was the only healthy lamb born out of hundreds of attempts.

Cloning has been an area of interest to scientists for centuries. Some animals and plants, and many bacteria, naturally produce genetically identical offspring. Komodo dragons are known sometimes to be able to produce fully grown adults from unfertilized eggs. In the human world, identical twins are technically also genetic clones, as they share DNA from a single fertilized egg that has split into two.

The first experiments with nuclear transfer took place as far back as 1928 on amphibian embryos. However, experiments with Dolly now provide proof that identical clones can be developed from ordinary adult cells—a breakthrough scientists have been striving for over decades.

Scientists are now discussing using the cloning process to protect endangered species, or even to "revive" extinct species. Others are considering how cloning might be used to develop human organs for transplant. By growing replacement organs from the recipient's own genetic material, they would be much less likely to be rejected by the immune system.

Fukushima: atomic future in disarray

BY OUR NUCLEAR CORRESPONDENT,
Fukushima, Japan, April 11, 2011

THE NUCLEAR CATASTROPHE at the Fukushima Daiichi power plant has been officially declared the world's worst nuclear accident since the Chernobyl disaster, in Ukraine, where an explosion on April 26, 1986 spread large quantities of radioactive particles into the atmosphere over much of western Russia and Europe.

Several countries, including Japan and Germany, are now reevaluating their long-term nuclear energy

strategies after a magnitude-9 earthquake struck off the east coast of Japan last month, triggering a 40-foot-high tsunami that washed over the east coast of Japan. The giant wave flooded three of the Fukushima Daiichi power station's six nuclear reactors, triggering a release of toxic radioactive waste. Some experts say it could take up to 100 years to completely clean up the site.

Nuclear energy was first used for domestic power generation in Arco, Idaho, in 1955. Since then, nuclear power has become one of the biggest sources of energy—one of the world's largest consumers being Japan, which, until the recent disaster, generated 30 percent of its electricity from nuclear power.

Some experts argue that nuclear power is essential to cut carbon emissions and reduce global warming. Others claim nuclear power is too risky to run and relies on reactors that are hugely expensive to get rid of at the end of their working life. There is also the question of how to safely store radioactive waste.

Stephen Tetlow, head of the Institution of Mechanical Engineers in London, says the disaster in Japan sends a clear challenge to aspiring scientists and engineers all over the world. "What we urgently need is a new generation of ingenious minds to ensure the well-being of planet, life, and people in the future."

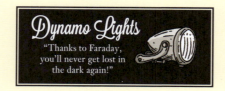

Your dinner is in the Petri dish!

New technique allows scientists to grow meat in a laboratory, leading some experts to claim that it will help solve the problems of global hunger and climate change

BY OUR SCIENCE EDITOR,
Amsterdam, Holland, August 6, 2013

WOULD YOU eat a hamburger grown in a lab? Food critics did just that yesterday, after they were served a "Frankenburger" made entirely from cow muscle cells grown by a team of Dutch scientists.

The tasters reported that the artificial burger tasted quite like meat, though not as juicy because it did not contain any fat cells. One critic said that if she hadn't been told, she would not have been able to tell it from the real thing.

Why would scientists want to create a test-tube burger? Dr. Mark Post, the head of the project, believes the lab-produced dinner offers a solution to a number of global problems with meat production. These largely relate to the alarming scale and inefficiency of meat production across the globe, where more than 70 percent of farmable land is currently used to raise livestock.

During this process animals consume more food than they produce for

humans to eat, and they also drink vast amounts of water. Dr. Post says moving meat production away from farms would free land for growing the staple foods that starving people really need—a potential way to feed present and future generations.

Lab-grown meat also bypasses many of the serious environmental problems that are associated with meat and dairy farming. Cows are notoriously gassy creatures, and livestock generate a fifth of all greenhouse gases, such as methane and carbon dioxide, warming up the atmosphere and contributing to climate change.

Dr. Post's hamburgers avoid these environmental hazards because they are grown directly from stem cells in laboratory conditions. They also avoid

the need to kill animals. The meat-growing process uses special stem cells taken from cow muscle, which can produce an almost limitless quantity of ordinary muscle cells—a single stem cell could conceivably make thousands of pounds of meat.

As the muscle cells multiply they are attached to anchor points, which makes them arrange themselves into fibers, much as though they were attached to a bone. This is what gives the cells their meaty texture.

But meat produced commercially in this way is not likely to be common very soon. At the moment, producing enough meat for a single burger takes about eight weeks, which means the stem cell burger currently comes with a hefty $280,000 price tag.

But, according to Dr. Post, it is only a matter of time before the process becomes cheaper and easier than raising cattle in a field.

"We can envisage households growing everything from tuna to ostrich at home in their own personal kitchen-incubators," he predicted.

Water jets from icy-moon Europa electrify search for extraterrestrial life

BY OUR SPACE EDITOR,
Pasadena, California, September 26, 2016

STUNNING IMAGES from the Hubble Space telescope have revealed plumes of water vapor are being expelled 125 miles into space from near the south pole of Europa, Jupiter's sixth moon. Europa has long been considered a possible place to look for signs of extraterrestrial life.

Europa is similar in size to our own Moon, but it is so far from the Sun that its surface is always under -260°F. With a range of chemicals from Europa's rocky center, energy from the tidal forces, and, above all, water, this moon is thought to have everything necessary to sustain forms of microbial life.

Plans to send probes to drill down to the hidden iced-over ocean have been considered. However, the engineering difficulties of landing on Europa's surface and drilling through perhaps miles of ice are immense.

NASA is considering plans to send probes to Europa in the 2020s to

examine many features of the moon, and these may now include attempts to collect material from the plumes to discover whether there is indeed life in the planet's watery interior. The challenges still remain daunting. Spacecraft can only make brief flybys of Europa; if they stay too long, they

would be fried by Jupiter's intense radiation. This same destructive energy would quickly break down any remains of life in the plumes.

Microorganisms are the most likely forms of life to be found in Europa's seas. As more becomes known of the solar system, the search for life is widening and now includes Earth's near neighbors Mars and Venus.

Oceans may exist not only on Europa but also on two of Jupiter's other moons: Callisto and Ganymede. "I want to go fishing on these icy moons of Jupiter, especially Europa," says Neil deGrasse Tyson, Frederick P. Rose Director of the American Museum of Natural History's Hayden Planetarium. "Every place on Earth where there's liquid water there's life, so your next round of questions is: is there life on these objects?"

A selection of letters from would-be readers down the ages

PRINTING PRESS—1450

Traditional crafts now under threat

HAVING WORKED my whole life copying great works of literature from across the ages, I was alarmed to read your recent piece on the new printing technology being developed by Mr. Gutenberg. The effect his new machine may have on the working lives of many ordinary people worries me deeply.

Our industry provides work not only to us scribes but also to livestock farmers, who provide animal skins for writing on, and to the woodcarvers, who produce print blocks.

Is it really worth sacrificing the livelihoods of all these people for the wider availability of reading material offered by Mr. Gutenberg's machine?

STERLING SKRIPTOR

Spreading the word

I WAS INTRIGUED to read about Mr. Gutenberg's printing machine because it is without a doubt the most exciting invention of our age. We live in a time of remarkable social, scientific, and theological changes and this new machine will allow these ideas to reach everyone.

As a man of science myself, this new device should allow me and my colleagues to develop and publish our ideas more easily.

I envision that there will soon be similar presses all across Europe, offering individuals everywhere the opportunity to broaden their minds and improve their lives. No gift could be more welcome!

SEBASTIANO SCIENZIATO

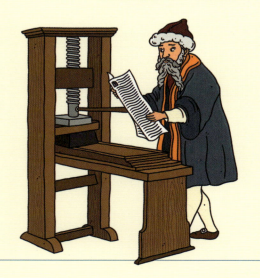

Who reads wins

AFTER READING your article on the new printing press designed by Mr. Gutenberg, I was surprised by the confidence with which your correspondent proclaimed that it might spur an intellectual revolution in Europe.

Only a meager proportion of the population is able to read, let alone understand the ideas contained within the works that will soon be rolling off the press. Society should put its faith in improving education, offering at least a basic level to all, if it truly wants to get us all reading.

PAUL PROFESSEUR

STEAM POWER—1781

Curse these iron horses

READING YOUR recent article on Mr. Watt's new engine, it is clear to me that this machine will pose a dire threat to the established social order as his steam-powered monsters choke up the countryside, forcing ordinary people to move to squalid new towns and cities in search of work.

And who benefits from this new development? Only the capitalists and the factory owners. The working man now faces the dual nightmares of harsh working hours and conditions, and deadly diseases bred from insanitary living standards. Wages are already beginning to drop, since these new machines have no need for skilled craftsmen. The government should put a stop to the relentless march of industry before disgruntled workers start fighting back.

DOMINIC DISGRUNTLED

VACCINATION—1796

Outrageous risk to innocent boy!

AS A DEVOTED mother myself, I was shocked by the questionable methods related in your article regarding the recent discoveries of Dr. Edward Jenner, namely his decision to use a young boy as a test subject.

I am left in a permanent state of confusion as to why he did not choose to make himself the victim of his reckless experimenting. The only answer I have is that he was too afraid his largely unfounded claims might prove fatal, and chose to put the life of a child at risk instead.

I do hope that this thoughtless approach does not become the norm in scientific circles.

FIONA FURIOUS

We have a cure!

READING YOUR ARTICLE on the extraordinary vaccination technique devised by Dr. Edward Jenner filled me with hope and excitement over the rewards daring scientists offer to society in the future.

In my opinion, Dr. Jenner should be congratulated on his tireless pursuit of this discovery, which could change so many lives across the globe for the better.

Dr. Jenner took risks, but not without first using his sharp mind and calm reasoning to predict the results, and for that we have all been given a medical innovation that may save the lives of millions.

IRINA IMPRESSED

EVOLUTION—1859

Where's the evidence?

MR. DARWIN should be congratulated for his ingenious theory about how living things in the natural world are adapted to different environments.

However, much of what he says seems to me to be pure speculation. When Mr. Darwin observes differences between species, he says that is because they live in different places, so they have "adapted." But what underlying mechanism does he think is responsible for causing creatures mysteriously to morph from one species into another?

Until he can answer that question—with real evidence to back up his ideas—I have to say his words should be treated with a good dose of doubt!

SALLY SKEPTIC

To comment on any issues in this book—visit whatonearthbooks.com/science

Darwin debate must be rational

AFTER READING your fine report on the latest work from Mr. Darwin, I quickly picked up a copy at my local bookstore and, I must say, it proved to be a most fascinating read. Mr. Darwin has clearly worked tirelessly on his theory and gone to great lengths to support his claims.

The significance of his work for all fields that deal with the past and where we came from is beyond words.

While I see a sea change on the horizon for the academic disciplines, in every field from biology to philosophy, it is clear that some people will find his theories entirely unpalatable.

I only hope that any debate is conducted reasonably and without recourse to conventional thought, as warrants a set of theories as exciting and controversial as Mr. Darwin's.

OCTAVIA OBSERVATIE

NOBEL PRIZE—1962

De-coding discovery

CONGRATULATIONS to James Watson, Francis Crick, and Maurice Wilkins for winning the Nobel Prize in Physiology or Medicine.

Their discovery of the structure of deoxyribonucleic acid, or DNA, which contains the instructions on how living things function and grow, is perhaps the greatest discovery about life on Earth since Charles Darwin's evolutionary theory.

As each living creature's DNA is unique, it means any material left at a crime scene, such as skin tissue or saliva, may one day help identify suspects. And that could be well worth a second prize, in my opinion!

EVERET B. ERNEST JR.

Unacceptable discrimination!

I WAS INFURIATED when I realized Rosalind Franklin was excluded from the Nobel Prize awarded to her colleagues: Wilkins, Crick and Watson. Without Dr. Franklin's pioneering work with X-ray crystallography no one would know how DNA works and the others would never have won the prize!

It makes a mockery of honoring contributions to humanity if one as important as hers is ignored. The Nobel Foundation's claim she was left out because she died four years ago simply isn't good enough—the committee ought to be ashamed!

AYLA-MAE AGGRIEVED

NUCLEAR POWER—2011

Nuclear power better for climate change

WHILE THERE ARE many lessons to be learned from the tragic Fukushima disaster, those who are more frightened than ever about nuclear energy should remember that the energy future of the world rests upon finding a practical solution to our ever-growing needs.

Renewable power cannot supply the vast amount of energy the world consumes, and traditional fossil fuels have been shown to pollute the atmosphere. Meanwhile, we wait anxiously for the moment when our reserves of coal, oil, and gas are either all spent or too dangerous to extract from the ground.

A nuclear future is the only viable future if we want to avoid the far more significant environmental and social disasters the alternatives present.

OLIVIA OPTIMISTA

No! to nuclear

THE FUKUSHIMA DISASTER is a wake-up call for the rest of the world. As members of the Green movement have repeatedly shown, nuclear power only offers the potential for disaster. Governments in search of an alternative to fossil fuels should look to renewable technology for a safer, more sustainable option.

Nuclear power is a ticking time bomb just waiting for the next disaster to occur. It is time that the world said "no" to this dangerous technology once and for all.

KWAN CONCERNED

SYNTHETIC FOOD—2013

No easy answers to global hunger issues

DR. POST IS NAIVE if he believes this bizarre "burger science" can really offer a solution to global hunger. Food shortages have dogged humanity since the dawn of time, and despite numerous advances science has repeatedly failed to save the most vulnerable nations from the problem.

By waiting for some kind of scientific innovation, we are neglecting the very real roots of the problem and forgetting the unforeseen consequences to our own health. We need to encourage agricultural development worldwide, confront corrupt governments, and campaign for more effective support from richer nations.

AHMED AGRICULTURE

Can't wait to fry it out!

EXPECT ME TO BE FIRST in line when the Frankenburger Bar opens, because I can't wait to try one of Dr. Post's creations!

With enough support, this lab-grown meat could become a global phenomenon, breaking the back of hunger and staving off environmental catastrophe as well. The prospect of skipping the grocery store and growing my own dinner at home fills me with sheer delight!

FREYA FRYER

See how many of our brain-teasing science & engineering questions you can answer...

MATH & MEASUREMENT

1. Babylonian mathematicians devised a counting system based on the number:
   a) 5
   b) 10
   c) 20
   d) 60

2. Euclid is famous for detailing which branch of mathematics?
   a) Algebra
   b) Calculus
   c) Arithmetic
   d) Geometry

3. Italian merchant Leonardo of Pisa is famous for introducing what to Europe?
   a) The compass
   b) Arabic numerals
   c) The abacus
   d) Oranges

4. The supercomputer that defeated chess grandmaster Garry Kasparov was called:
   a) True Blue
   b) Big Blue
   c) Blue Brother
   d) Deep Blue

5. Pierre de Fermat and Blaise Pascal pioneered the mathematics of probability by:
   a) Throwing dice
   b) Flipping coins
   c) Tossing pancakes
   d) Playing Russian roulette

6. Who developed Colossus, the world's first fixed-program digital computer?
   a) Alan Turing
   b) Albert Einstein
   c) Tommy Flowers
   d) James Chadwick

7. In which unit of measurement does water boil at 100° and freeze at 0°?
   a) Celsius
   b) Fahrenheit
   c) Kelvin
   d) Richter

PHYSICS & CHEMISTRY

8. Chinese monks, who were trying to concoct a potion for everlasting life, accidentally made:
   a) Gunpowder
   b) Chili powder
   c) Curry powder
   d) Custard powder

9. Which of the following scientists won two Nobel prizes?
   a) Marie Curie
   b) Florence Nightingale
   c) Ada Lovelace
   d) Rachel Carson

10. The first atomic device was nicknamed:
    a) The Inspector
    b) The Gadget
    c) The Trinity
    d) The Daisy

11. The Higgs boson is a subatomic particle thought to be responsible for:
    a) Gravity
    b) Mass
    c) Electricity
    d) Light

12. Friedrich Wöhler pioneered the science of organic chemistry by artificially synthesizing which naturally occurring substance?
    a) Nicotine
    b) Aspirin
    c) Penicillin
    d) Urea

13. William Whewell is famous for coining the term:
    a) Scientist
    b) Technician
    c) Engineer
    d) Geek

14. Leyden jars were sometimes used for which of the following procedures:
    a) Removing eye cataracts
    b) Storing blood during bloodletting
    c) Stemming blood during surgery
    d) Electrocuting bad servants and children

MEDICINE & BIOLOGY

15. According to the Ancient Greek theory of disease, which of the following was NOT one of the four bodily humors?
    a) Blood
    b) Bile
    c) Water
    d) Phlegm

16. Alexander Fleming discovered the anti-bacterial properties of *Penicillium* after:
    a) Not washing his Petri dishes
    b) Knocking over a box of athlete's foot powder
    c) Illicitly cultivating magic mushrooms
    d) Sneezing into a batch of brewer's yeast

17. Italian inventor Evangelista Torricelli invented a primitive:
    a) Thermometer
    b) Barometer
    c) Compass
    d) Calculator

18. Which of the following statements about the pH scale is NOT true?
    a) Substances with a pH < 7 are acidic
    b) Substances with a pH > 7 are alkaline
    c) The pH scale is linear not logarithmic
    d) The color for highly acidic substances is red

19. What did Robert Boyle put in his vacuum pump to see whether it survived without air?
    a) A lark
    b) A pigeon
    c) A robin
    d) A dodo

20. Which of the following blood groups was NOT one of those identified by Austrian biologist Karl Landsteiner?
    a) A
    b) B
    c) O
    d) R

21. Physician Joseph Lister is famous for pioneering which of the following?
    a) Antibiotics
    b) Antiseptics
    c) Antibodies
    d) Antidisestablishmentarianism

22. Dr. Edward Jenner is famous for:
    a) Electrocuting a dead frog
    b) Deliberately infecting an eight-year-old boy with smallpox
    c) Amputating his own arm
    d) Inventing the electric lightbulb

EARTH & LAND

23. Chinese scholar Zhang Heng is famous for inventing a device that could:
    a) Point south
    b) Detect earthquakes
    c) Magnify images
    d) Glow in the dark

24. According to Leonardo da Vinci, fossils are found high up in rocks because:
    a) Ancient people put them there
    b) The ancient seafloor has been pushed up to a new level
    c) The seas once covered all the Earth
    d) They originally fell from the sky

25. What do plants release during photosynthesis, as discovered by Dutch botanist Jan Ingenhousz?
    a) Water
    b) Carbon dioxide
    c) Sunlight
    d) Oxygen

All the correct answers can be found somewhere in this book!

26. Austrian monk Gregor Mendel is famous for discovering the laws of inheritance after cultivating:
a) 50,000 silkworms
b) 29,000 pea plants
c) 17,000 fruit flies
d) 9,000 Vietnamese bananas

27. *Duria Antiquior* is a famous:
a) Painting
b) Book
c) Sculpture
d) Spell

28. Who independently came up with a theory of evolution at the same time as Charles Darwin?
a) Charles Lyell
b) John James Audubon
c) Thomas Huxley
d) Alfred Russel Wallace

29. Which of the following rock types were NOT described by James Hutton:
a) Igneus
b) Oceanic
c) Sedimentary
d) Metamorphic

BUILDING & INVENTION

30. What accounts for what the Ancient Greeks saw when they rubbed amber against cloth?
a) Magnetism
b) Erosion
c) Static electricity
d) A genie

31. What did Greek genius Archimedes invent that allowed him to launch a ship single-handedly?
a) A crane
b) A slide
c) A pulley
d) A screw

32. A *polyspastos* was a human-powered:
a) Crane
b) Water pump
c) Clock
d) Submarine

33. King Henry VI of England was the first person to grant:
a) Stocks and shares
b) A patent
c) A pension
d) Three wishes

34. The discovery of which material in Cumbria, England, helped introduce the practice of writing and drawing?
a) Chalk
b) Oil
c) Graphite
d) Alum

35. Alfred Nobel, whose legacy led to the prestigious Nobel Prize, was also the inventor of:
a) The fountain pen
b) The traffic light
c) The gramophone
d) Dynamite

TRANSPORT & COMMUNICATIONS

36. Before they took to the skies, the Wright brothers were mechanics, specializing in making and repairing:
a) Sewing machines
b) Bicycles
c) Typewriters
d) Lawnmowers

37. The first commercial MAGLEV train was opened in which city?
a) Tokyo
b) Dallas
c) Sydney
d) Birmingham

38. The world's first supersonic car was called:
a) Blast
b) Thrash
c) Thrust
d) Bloodhound

39. For how many years was the supersonic airliner Concorde in active service?
a) 19
b) 27
c) 29
d) 32

40. John McAdam's revolutionary technique for road building became known as:
a) Macademics
b) Macadamization
c) Macadamorphic
d) Macadamandeve

41. Which of the following represents the letter W in Morse code?
a) * - *
b) - -*
c) * * -
d) * - -

42. Which creature was NOT included in the Montgolfier test balloon flight in September 1783?
a) Rooster
b) Rabbit
c) Sheep
d) Duck

43. Where did inventor Edmond Halley test out his experimental diving bell?
a) In a swimming pool
b) In Lake Michigan
c) In the River Thames
d) In a fishpond

SKY & SPACE

44. Greek thinker Aristarchus concluded that:
a) The Earth orbits the Sun
b) The Universe is a flat disc
c) Jupiter has four moons
d) The Earth is round

45. What did Greek philosopher Thales predict on May 28, 585 BC?
a) A solar eclipse
b) A lunar eclipse
c) A 9.0-magnitude earthquake
d) A tsunami

46. Ulugh Beg's giant sextant, built in his home city of Samarkand, could accurately measure:
a) The distance between the Earth and the Sun
b) The length of a year
c) The circumference of the Earth
d) The number of stars in the northern hemisphere

47. The opposite of a red giant is commonly known as a:
a) White elf
b) White hobbit
c) White pixie
d) White dwarf

48. The first living creature to be launched into Earth orbit was a dog called:
a) Lulu
b) Laika
c) Litva
d) Lolly

49. What was the name of the first Space Shuttle that blasted off from Cape Canaveral in 1981?
a) *Atlantis*
b) *Enterprise*
c) *Discovery*
d) *Columbia*

50. How long after Apollo's landing on the Moon did Neil Armstrong take his giant leap for mankind?
a) 30 minutes
b) 2 hours
c) 6 hours
d) 1 day

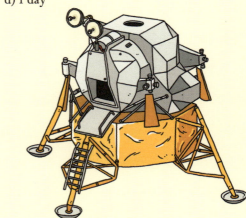

◆ Curiosity King

Christopher LLOYD

The Chronicler

Historian Christopher Lloyd graduated with a double-first class degree in history from Cambridge University. Christopher then became Science Correspondent with *The Sunday Times* newspaper in London. Now he is a best-selling author of more than 15 books on world history including *What on Earth Happened? The Complete Story of the Planet, Life, and People from the Big Bang to the Present Day* (Bloomsbury) and the series of What on Earth? timelines. He frequently gives talks at festivals and schools.

chris@whatonearthbooks.com

◆ What on Earth?

WHO ON EARTH ARE WE?

Here at What on Earth Publishing, we think that learning should always be fun.

Our timelines of nature, history, literature, science, and sport are designed to stimulate natural curiosity by connecting the dots of the past.

Wallbooks can be browsed like books or displayed as posters on a wall.

whatonearthbooks.com/about

◆ Master of Pens

ANDY FORSHAW

The Illustrator

Illustrator Andy Forshaw graduated with a BA in graphic design and illustration from London's Central St. Martins College. In 2010, Andy and Christopher teamed up to found What on Earth Publishing with a view to establishing new ways of making big history accessible to all ages. Andy has since individually created more than 5,000 illustrations that are featured in the range of What on Earth? timelines. When not illustrating, Andy can be found exploring the countryside on his bike.

andy@whatonearthbooks.com

---

❸ FANTASTIC FORMATS

OUR TIMELINES COME IN THREE FANTASTIC FORMATS

whatonearthbooks.com/shop

1 **WALLBOOKS** feature a six-foot timeline, plus a newspaper packed with stories, pictures, letters, and a quiz. Perfect for everyone.

2 **POSTERBOOKS** are a gigantic ten-foot version of the timeline, printed on heavy paper and laminated for extra durability. Perfect for schools.

3 **STICKERBOOKS** include around a hundred stickers, and a simplified 5-foot version of the timeline to stick them on to. Perfect for younger readers.

 AMERICAN MUSEUM OF NATURAL HISTORY

The **American Museum of Natural History** in New York City is one of the largest and most respected museums in the world, with an annual attendance of approximately 5 million.

Since the Museum was founded in 1869, its collections have grown to include more than 33 million specimens and artifacts relating to the natural world and human cultures.

The Museum showcases its collections in 45 exhibition halls, and, behind the scenes, approximately 200 scientists carry out cutting-edge research. Plan a trip to the Museum, home of the world's largest collection of dinosaur fossils, or visit online at amnh.org.

Central Park West at 79th Street, New York, NY 10024, USA

THE **WHAT ON EARTH?**  COLLECTION

1. Nature **2. Science** **3. Big History**

Written by **Christopher Lloyd** and **Patrick Skipworth**. Illustrated and designed by **Andy Forshaw**.
Published by What on Earth Publishing Ltd.
Wallbook is a registered trademark of What on Earth Publishing Ltd.
First published in the U.S. in 2017. First published in Great Britain in 2014. © 2014, 2017.

ISBN: 978-0-9932847-5-5
Dewey: 509
BISAC: JNF061010 JUVENILE NONFICTION / Technology / Inventions
JNF007030 JUVENILE NONFICTION / Science & Nature / History of Science
SCI034000 SCIENCE / History
LC Class: Q125
Science--History--Juvenile literature
Technology--History--Juvenile literature
Inventions--History--Juvenile literature

For information about U.S. distribution or bulk sales, please contact Ingram Publisher Services, Customer Service Box 631, 14 Ingram Blvd., La Vergne, TN 37086.
Telephone 866-400-5351 or email *ips@ingramcontent.com*.

www.whatonearthbooks.com